DEADLY

DEADLY DETECTIVES

To Wendy for bringing the Darke side,
and for being with us every step of the way.

DEADLY

DETECTIVES

STEVE BACKSHALL

First published in Great Britain in 2013
by Orion Children's Books
a division of the Orion Publishing Group Ltd
Orion House
5 Upper St Martin's Lane
London WC2H 9EA
An Hachette UK Company

1 3 5 7 9 10 8 6 4 2

A catalogue record for this book is available from the British Library.

Printed in Italy

www.orionbooks.co.uk

CONTENTS

The world of tracking will enrich your life beyond your wildest dreams, but any foray into the outdoors must be done with great care. If you are working by the coast, watch out for the tides and for ever-changing weather. Always go out prepared for the worst in terms of weather and temperature.

Make sure to wash your hands thoroughly immediately after handling skulls, bones and droppings. Do not handle droppings if you think they may be from a felid (member of the cat family).

If your tracking should lead you to the animal itself, then respect its personal space and be careful not to disturb it. Don't touch, poke or pick up animals, even if they appear to be dead.

Knives, machetes and fire are all essential tools for the outdoorsman to learn to use properly, but handle them very carefully. Too many budding naturalists have taken off the tip of a finger through careless use of a penknife. And remember that forest fires are all too easy to start and almost impossible to stop.

YOU'RE COMING WITH ME

Finding wildlife is rarely easy. It's true that sometimes you'll be at the seaside paddling around in the surf and a seal will pop up right in front of you, but most of the time you have to work for encounters worth having. The best way to increase your chances is to become a Sherlock Holmes of the natural world. Learn to look for signs that other people would wander straight past, and understand their hidden meaning.

I'm going to show you how to spot the fascinating clues in the natural world that can teach you so much about animal life – signs such as tracks, droppings and evidence of feeding activity. We'll track some animals close to home, then I'll take you with me to do some Deadly Detective work further afield.

There are some conundrums for you to solve yourself, as well as tales of the dazzling animal encounters that come from wild sleuthing.

Being aware of wildlife signs is exciting in itself, even if you never encounter the animals that left

A microscope is a powerful tool, offering a view into an otherwise hidden miniature world.

Tracking wildlife isn't always easy.

them. The wild world is alive with stories of animals that live their lives far from our prying eyes.

Some of the finest moments of my life have involved tracking. In the Himalayas we discovered male tiger tracks alongside a river, the first evidence that these rare cats lived in the region. In Venezuela, on top of a peak that had never been climbed before, we found paw prints that told of a mystery animal, almost certainly a new species, isolated there in the mountain mists, and I knew I would have to go back and explore further. These are experiences that I will always treasure, and you could have some of your own.

This book will span the globe, taking in every habitat, from Himalayan peaks to wave-blasted Pacific coasts, from shifting sands to sparkling snow. It'll give you the tools you need to track wildlife wherever you are on earth.

Steve

CHAPTER 1
TRACKING IN A WILD WORLD

Learning the basic elements of being a wildlife detective will change your life, and particularly your experience of being outside. Nothing beats the sensation of finding a track, musing: 'Hmmm, looks like fallow deer – a mother and fawn – moving slowly, probably grazing,' and then rounding a corner and seeing the animals themselves, your detective work proved right!

In order to succeed, you need to become the animal you're tracking, to see the world through its eyes, move as it does and visualise every step. There will be places where you cannot see any tracks, and then you will have to feel instinctively where your quarry would choose to go.

Something as simple as learning a few common bird calls means that you will never be alone in the natural world. It's like learning another language. You become aware of a thousand conversations going on in the bushes and trees as you walk through your local woodland, and what you'll realise is that the birds are talking about you behind your back.

A snow leopard.

THE ORIGINS OF TRACKING

Despite all the joy that tracking can give the modern naturalist, the skills themselves are ancient. Tracking developed among hunter-gatherer peoples, enabling them to find animals they would eventually kill and eat. For them, reading nature's clues could mean the difference between life and death.

Even today, the finest trackers are those who rely on it for their livelihood. The San peoples of the Kalahari are able to detect so much from the tracks of antelope that they can pick out an animal with a tiny injury that might make it vulnerable.

Hunters in the Kalahari following a trail.

When they've found a likely target, they'll run after it for many hours, refusing to allow their prey animal any rest, until in many cases it simply dies of exhaustion. These Kalahari hunters are better than their four-legged prey at regulating their body heat through sweating. There's an interesting theory that this method of endurance hunting could have led to our caveman ancestors losing their body hair and starting to walk upright on two legs.

I've been on the hunt with the Penan tribe in Borneo, stalking riverbeds for tracks of mouse deer, wild pig or birds, which they dispatch with a dart from a long, crafted blowpipe.

In Australia, a wizened Aboriginal 'uncle' took me tracking wallabies, stopping at precise bushes to dig up witchetty grubs – the burrowing larvae of a moth, usually eaten raw, which taste a bit like runny scrambled eggs! We also found honey ants which store sweet nectar in the abdomens of special individuals called 'repletes' that hang inside their nests; they taste like sugar candy. The Aboriginal man's ability to read the world around him was enviable, but his snoring at night could have woken the dead!

A witchetty grub.

Every time I'm in Africa I follow game reserve wardens around like a bad smell, nagging them with my incessant questions and asking them to share their knowledge. They become so familiar with the animals on their patch that they can tell the exact story of every creature merely from a print or two. It's a skill I envy terribly and will never tire of studying. And it doesn't just happen in exotic climes. The gillies in Scotland

When tracking mammals or birds, I wear a camouflage suit
to help me stay out of sight.

Rutting red deer stags.

are gamekeepers who can approach within yards of rutting red deer stags without the animals noticing their presence. Tracking skills are just as useful to me back home in the UK as they are in far-flung places.

Many clues only last days or hours, but this is not always the case. Fossilised footprints of long-extinct animals still exist and reading these tracks has helped palaeontologists to

Fossilised animal tracks in the Namib Desert.

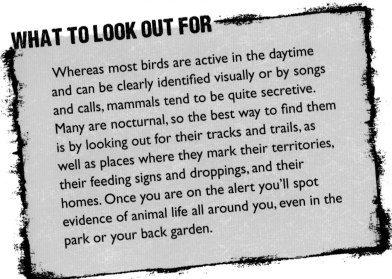

WHAT TO LOOK OUT FOR

Whereas most birds are active in the daytime and can be clearly identified visually or by songs and calls, mammals tend to be quite secretive. Many are nocturnal, so the best way to find them is by looking out for their tracks and trails, as well as places where they mark their territories, their feeding signs and droppings, and their homes. Once you are on the alert you'll spot evidence of animal life all around you, even in the park or your back garden.

recreate a world we will never see again. Perhaps our ancient ancestors followed these same signs, grunting to each other as they drew closer to a woolly mammoth, ready to do battle with the mighty beast in order to feed their clan.

Track and trails

When an animal steps into a favourably soft surface or substrate, it leaves behind an impression of its foot – a track. The best surfaces for tracks are shallow, firm snow, damp (but not too soggy) sand or mud with a fine grain, and soft dusty ground. A track can tell you what species the animal is, possibly its size and maybe even its sex. A line of these tracks in sequence, combined with other signs, is known as a trail.

A trail, though, is the real treasure for any Deadly Detective. A good naturalist can look at a trail and know how many animals have passed through, what speed they were moving at and what their intentions were. The trail may lead to the animal's prey, its home or even an encounter with the animal itself.

An otter track in wet sand. The print is quite crisp and clear, even the shallowest claw marks are still visible, suggesting this is a fresh track.

Taking a closer look at the perfect prints left by a bobcat.

Lighting makes a big difference to viewing a footprint. Midday sunlight directly overhead can bleach a print out. The lower light early or late in the day is much better. At night, instead of shining your torch straight down into a print, kneel down alongside it and angle your torchlight across the top. This creates shadows and makes the print more evident. If you have a good deep print in nice silty sand or mud, a plaster or polymorph cast can be taken which will give you an excellent impression to be studied later. If you find a good print, you might like to sketch or photograph it and also measure it so that you can record all the details.

Q. *What do you think could have made these prints?*

A. These are classic dog tracks, and have been made by a coyote running across the dunes, probably hunting for rabbits.

Q. Why are these prints all upside down, standing up above the snow rather than having been pressed into it?

A. These prints were made by a coyote. The animal's weight pressed down on the snow, compressing it – making it more compact. As wind blew away surface snow, and it started to melt in the sunshine, the compacted snow lasted longer, leaving the prints standing up above the baseline, in relief.

TYPES OF MAMMAL FOOT

Learning about the different kinds of animal feet will help you identify tracks and trails. There are three main types.

Plantigrade
Human beings, bears and badgers are all plantigrade mammals: they walk on the sole of the foot. Depending on the depth of the marks, almost all of the foot will be represented in a track and you may be able to see toe pads and claws. Most insectivores such as hedgehogs and shrews are also plantigrades.

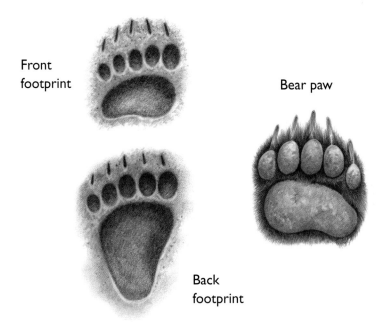

Front footprint

Bear paw

Back footprint

Digitigrade
Cats and dogs are digitigrade mammals: they walk and run on their toes. Digitigrade animals often spend a lot of time in full sprint and their foot position helps this. The print will show most or all of the toe pads and palm pads. Dogs also leave claw

marks, but most cats retract their claws so they don't show in prints. Often the thumb does not appear in the print as it is positioned higher up the leg.

Lion footprint

Lion paw

Unguligrade

These animals effectively walk on their toenails, creating tracks known as slots. Classic unguligrades include deer, pigs and antelope. The other toes (dewclaws) may have migrated up the foot, and may only show in very deep prints.

Cattle footprint

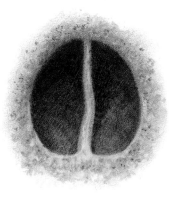

Cattle foot

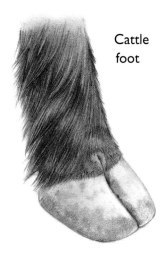

Q. *What animals do you think made these three tracks?*

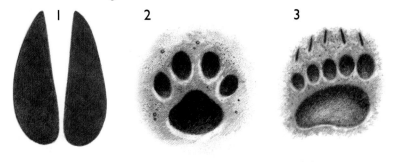

| | | |
| 1 | 2 | 3 |

A. 1 Deer. 2 Cat. 3 Bear.

Other animals

It's not only mammals that leave tracks. You will often see bird tracks in mud or sand, and these can help you identify the species. Most birds have four toes – three pointing forwards and one back – but some have only three toes, or one higher up the leg which does not appear in tracks. Reptiles, including snakes, also leave signs of their movements, and even insects may leave a trail in soft surfaces.

Gait

Gait is the style of movement. Human beings have several gaits, from a gentle stroll to a full-on sprint. Our tracks and trails depend on which we are using, and animals are no different.

Walking

As an animal walks, only one foot is lifted from the floor at any one time. Strides are short, and you may well get registration (foot in foot, the hind foot being placed into the track of the fore foot). You can almost sense the ease and leisure of the animal as it moves.

Trotting and running

The stride length of a trotting animal is longer and opposite legs are lifted at the same time, so there is a greater distance between the tracks. There may be distortion in the tracks themselves, and the prints become deeper with the greater impact.

Full gallop

When an animal gallops it will take all four feet off the ground at the same time at some points, making it completely airborne. Tracks are very deep and the stride length is even longer than in a trotting trail.

Bounds and hopping

In a gallop the main drive comes from the front feet, but in a bound the power comes from the rear feet. There may be extra marks left by other parts of the body such as the tail.

A PILE OF POO!

Poo is also known as droppings or scat and it can tell you a great deal about an animal's life. The dryness and smell of a dropping (taking the weather and temperature into consideration) can tell you how recently the animal was there. The dropping's contents reveal a great deal about what the animal was feeding on. A vast dropping the size of a football, full of undigested grasses and leaves, has come out of the bottom of a very big herbivore such as an elephant. Longer thinner droppings laced with feathers, bones or teeth are typical of carnivores such as foxes or cats.

Apart from foxes, most animals that live in dens take care to leave their droppings outside their home. Badgers create concentrated latrines, which also serve to mark the boundaries of their territories. Look out for piles of black greasy droppings that may have the remnants of prey such as beetle wing cases inside them.

Some birds produce very liquid droppings, while others have round or cylindrical poo. You may see the remains of the hard external parts of insects in the droppings of insect-eating birds, or there may be undigested berries or seeds. Birds such as owls, gulls and crows also get rid of food they cannot digest by coughing up neatly packed little pellets containing fur, feathers, shells and so on. These tell us a great deal about that bird's diet.

Always take great care when investigating poo. With carnivore droppings, particularly, use a stick or wear disposable gloves. Always wash your hands well after handling any kind of droppings.

Q. *What animals do you think made these three piles of poo?*

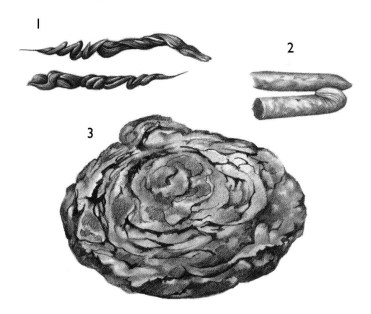

A. 1 Weasel. 2 Woodpecker. 3 Cow.

THE CASE OF:

THE GIANT
SCOLOPENDRA
AND THE VAMPIRE BAT

When I first heard of the existence of a giant centipede
that caught and ate bats, I knew that someday I would have
to film it. However, a fire raged through the cave system
where this had been seen happening, so I lost track of the
story for many years.

In 2010, Lizzie, one of the Deadly 60 researchers,
traced a scientist working in Venezuela who had
discovered a new cave where the centipedes lived.
When we arrived at the cave, we instantly went on the
search for signs. One of the first traces I found was a pile
of smeary black droppings on the cave floor that looked
to me like lumps of congealed blood. I looked up to see
an alcove in the ceiling filled with bats – vampire bats!

We scoured the cave, looking in every single crack and
cranny, but had no luck finding centipedes. The next evening
we came back and after hours of searching the sound
recordist Simon yelled, 'There's one!' And there it was,
a centipede as long as my forearm. I took it in my hand
(wearing a thick gardening glove), and it was stronger for
its size than any other creature I've ever handled.

Grotesque, ghastly, gripping.

Animal bones

Bones, particularly skulls, can tell you an enormous amount about animals. The dentition, or how the teeth are arranged, is very different in carnivores and herbivores. Carnivores tend to have long, sharp curved canine teeth that do the job of killing their prey, then stout carnassials or cheek teeth further back down the jaw for the business of munching it up. Herbivores (plant eaters) have large flattened molars for grinding down plant food.

Deer skull (herbivore)

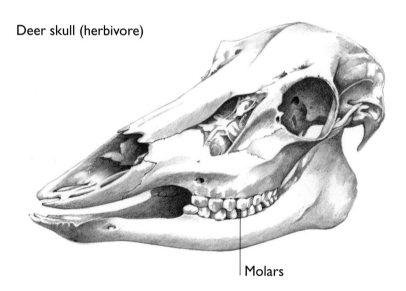

Molars

You are most likely to find skulls from smaller animals, but every once in a while you may come across whole skeletons from larger beasts. Large crests over the top of the skull (sagittal crest) and big cheekbones (zygomatic arches) are a sign of animals with a large bite force.

Rat skull (rodent)

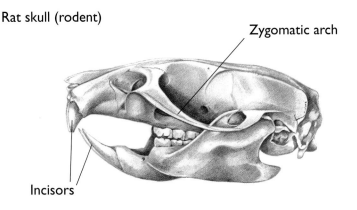

Zygomatic arch

Incisors

Animals such as hyenas that crunch clear through the bone of carcasses have the biggest zygomatic arches. I once found something really interesting when I compared the skull of a polar bear which had lived its life in a zoo to others in the wild. The wild bears, which had obviously spent their lives munching seals and whales, had vast sagittal crests. The one from captivity barely had one at all . . .

Lynx skull (carnivore)

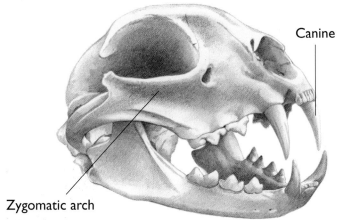

Canine

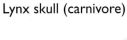
Zygomatic arch

Animal homes

You might think that all animals have permanent homes that they return to every night (or day) and stay in all the time. However, this is rarely true. Birds only use nests to raise their young, and roost elsewhere for the rest of their lives. Most birds build a nest afresh every season, but a few use the same nest and add to it over generations. Bald eagle nests, for example, can be as much as six metres deep and weigh over a ton. Nests are very different for good reason. If all birds were to hide their nests behind loose chunks of tree bark, as treecreepers do, then it would be a simple matter for predators to find and raid them all.

Bald eagle on its nest.

This is a classic rabbit burrow entrance.

Animals that tunnel may well make their homes conspicuous by throwing out the excavated earth on to the surface. This is particularly noticeable in areas where there is sandy or chalky

A badger's sett, I am kneeling on the spoil pile.

soil. Look at the entrance for evidence as to whether or not the burrow is in use: fresh paw prints and strong animal scents are a good sign, while old dusty cobwebs over the hole are not. A rabbit's warren is an interconnected maze of tunnels with many entrances. There will be many small round droppings about.

A badger's sett is often marked out by huge amounts of excavated earth and lots of different entrances, not all of which will be in use. Some of these complexes can be used for decades. Look out for characteristic black and white hairs, obvious paths made by the low-slung body of heavy male badgers, and bits of nesting material that may have been cleared out of the sett or dropped on the way in. If you really want to see whether a badger is using the sett, put a doormat of flour or sand outside the entrance on a dry evening. Next day, you may well be rewarded with a glorious line of badger prints.

This log has been torn apart by badgers in search of beetle grubs.

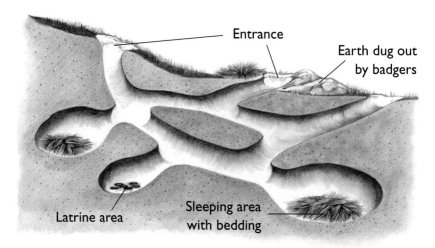

Entrance

Earth dug out by badgers

Latrine area

Sleeping area with bedding

A fox's den or earth may be marked by the fan-shaped spoil pile outside it. It is often dug into a bank, and the entrance may be deceptively small. Footprints, food remains and that pungent foxy pong are all a good sign that fantastic Mr Fox is home. Interestingly, the droppings and urine of foxes contain nutrients that plants love. In spring there may be much lusher vegetation growing around the entrances to fox and badger holes. This is because their droppings and prey remains contain nitrates – essentially fertiliser!

Squirrels build a nest known as a drey high up in a tree. It's often circular, with a roof and a tunnel-like entrance, and is positioned close to the tree trunk.

Some mammals build dens in the winter where they hibernate or raise their young, but for the rest of the year they just curl up somewhere inconspicuous out of the weather. Deer, antelope and hares do not have regular places to lay their heads, but will lay up in temporary forms or rest sites. They rarely return to the same site again.

THE CASE OF:

THE BURMESE PYTHON

This is excellent evidence of quite how much can be learned from finding out what animals eat, whether by studying poo, pellets or stomach contents.

All the above prey items were found in the stomachs of invasive Burmese pythons in Florida's Everglades. These snakes were once pets that either escaped or were released into the wild by their owners, and they are now starting to take over!

Here you can see the skull of a heron, hoof and fur from a white-tailed deer, a claw and fur from a bobcat, and scales from a two-metre alligator! All of these animals had been eaten by very big snakes that should not have been in the swamps in the first place.

FEEDING SIGNS

Be on the look out for signs of animals' feeding habits. You may spot stripped branches, torn bark, evidence of digging and even a carcass. If you come across the remains of a decent-sized mammal, such as a deer, there is much you can learn about the predator from the way the carcass has been killed and eaten. Prints and feeding signs do not necessarily come from the predator that made the kill; even some of the biggest and most powerful beasts are not averse to eating carrion (animals that are already dead).

Rabbits have been eating the bark of this tree.

Foxes usually take small and medium-sized prey. Their jaws are not strong enough to kill a larger animal outright. In extreme cases, they may take larger prey, but the kill will have taken time – there will be extensive signs of the struggle, and the prey animal will carry many smaller wounds.

The wolverine is often known as 'the glutton'. They bite at the heels of some large animals, and will leap towards the throat of others. Wolverines slice up their prey, hoarding items such as the head and entrails under rocks or snow. They are great climbers, and may even drag chunks of their kill up trees.

If the carcass is mostly whole, apart from the eaten sections, it could well be the work of a cat. The throat and nose area may show wounds or bruising. In Norway, we found a deer that had

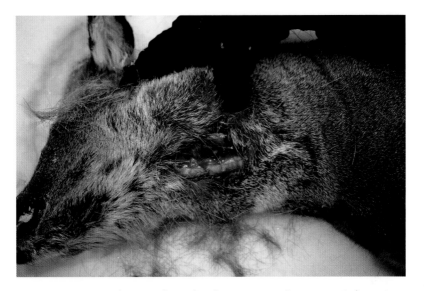

The wounds on this deer suggest it has been killed by a lynx.

been killed by a large lynx and when we looked under the fur we saw small puncture marks around the larynx. The first feeding had begun around the shoulders. These marks are also classic sign of a mountain lion, bobcat or leopard kill. Mountain lions (also known as cougars or pumas) will often bury their kills; lynx rarely do so. None of these cats are fond of carrion, preferring live food.

Bears usually kill their prey with a smashing blow from one of their front paws. The spine and/or skull may be brutally broken. Bears feed on the chest area of mammal prey first, and then the entrails. With salmon, they may rip out only the fatty chunk behind the head or neatly fillet the fish with a single tear of their muzzle. Kills are often at least partially buried. Look for scratch signs nearby, and very large and smelly scats. If you think you've found the remains of bear prey, leave the area IMMEDIATELY and do not make camp within at least half a mile. Bears can be very, very territorial around their kills.

A wolf kill is the most distinctive. A pack all grip the meat with their incisors and canines, brace themselves backwards against their huge front paws, then shake their heads from side to side to dislodge bits of meat. Blood goes everywhere. Wolves do not bury their kills; members of a pack can each eat several kilos of meat at a sitting so they rarely have anything left to cache. However, if the prey is too large to finish in one go, the wolves will probably wait and watch, then return to feed when it is safe and they are hungry again. They have very powerful jaws, so there will be bone fragments and cracked bones.

This photo shows the remnants of a wolf kill I found in Yellowstone National Park. It was a little tricky figuring out what had happened, as the kill site was several days old and so lots of animals had scavenged there. Indeed, we first found it because there were so many ravens in the trees nearby. There were tracks from coyotes, bald eagles, red fox and from the wolves themselves. After brushing away the top layer of snow, we saw that the layer underneath looked like a butcher's shop floor, stained red with blood. The lower jawbone of the elk that had been killed was nearby, picked completely clean, and part of the pelt had been dragged away by foxes.

The elk jawbone, found along with lots of blood and hair.

READING THE SKIES

Any Deadly Detective needs to be able to read the weather and understand the ways in which animal activities might be a sign of weather changes.

'Mackerel scales and mare's tails, tall ships trim their sails'.
These descriptions are of several formations caused by cirrus clouds, which are formed very high up by high-altitude winds. Wispy cirrus or cirrocumulus clouds usually signal that there will be a change in the weather. You might also see a halo around the sun or moon, caused by light bouncing through the ice crystals in those same high clouds.

'Red sky at night, sailor's delight;
red sky in the morning, sailor's warning.'

TOP TIPS FOR A DEADLY DETECTIVE: Kit

- Ruler or tape measure to measure tracks
- Pencil and notebook to record your observations
- Magnifying glass
- Plastic bags or collecting pots for any interesting finds
- Tweezers for picking up small items
- Disposable gloves
- Stick for pulling apart poo or pellets
- Camera
- Field guide

If the sky is red at night, the air to the west of you is clear enough for the sun's rays to shine through. Much of our weather in the UK comes from the west, so this is a sign that coming conditions are good. On the other hand, if the sky is red in the morning, it could be the first rays of dawn hitting cirrus clouds high up – a sign of a change in weather.

There is some evidence that swallows and other birds will fly higher when good weather is due. This is because of a change in pressure, which means their insect prey will be flying higher up. Also it may be that crickets and grasshoppers chirp slower in cold weather and faster when it's warm.

If you're lost at sea, look to the horizon. Clouds cluster around land, as wind and weather fronts form around solid ground. Now you might like to try some Deadly Detective work for yourself. You can start by looking for signs of life in your back garden or the local park while you build up your knowledge.

Clouds cluster around landmasses.

TOP TIPS FOR A DEADLY DETECTIVE:
Dos and don'ts

- Never touch or pick up poo or pellets with your bare hands. Use gloves or tweezers, and if you want to investigate poo, do this with a stick.
- Don't touch any dead animals you might find.
- Watch out for prickly or stinging plants, including poison ivy.
- Look out for ticks which can bite, and also stinging insects such as bees and wasps.
- Most important of all, never approach animals too closely. Always keep your distance.

CHAPTER 2
ANCIENT WOODLAND

Few environments have as much magic for me as a twisted oak or beech wood, where each tree could have been standing since Shakespeare was writing his sonnets. A mature oak may be home to as many as 600 different species of animal, from tiny spiders to goldfinches that weave spider web silk into their nests. In the spring, as bluebells and wild garlic bloom, such woodlands ring with the tunes of birds advertising themselves to mates. It's a place that's full of wonder, a paradise for the Deadly Detective.

Quite often mammals will follow a set pattern through their day, and the habits of some creatures will fundamentally alter their environment. If you see a field with bushes round the outside all trimmed to the same height, as if a gardener has been around with a hedge trimmer, it's likely that deer browse here; they have clipped the bushes to the exact height they can

Can you spot the deer line on this row of trees and bushes?

This path through the woods has been made by animals such as deer.

Black and white hairs caught on barbed wire are a sure sign of badgers.

reach. If a woodland trail goes under a barbed wire fence, or under a log that is too low for a human, dog or deer to stoop beneath, examine the wood or wire. You may find the presence of black and white hairs – the telltale sign that the path was made by badgers.

Moles have been at work here.

47

Q. *what did this?*

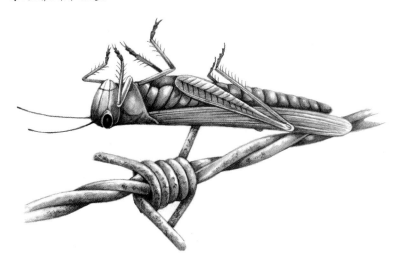

A. This is the work of a shrike. They impale their prey on these spikes, or, more likely with the great grey shrike, wedge them into the angle of twigs in order to tear them apart. This is why shrikes are also known as 'butcher birds'.

Dog or fox?

The most important thing with tracking is to know what the most common prints are likely to be in a certain area. In a suburban backyard, you should look at a feline print and think cat, not Bengal tiger! In British woodland, you're more likely to encounter prints of domestic dogs than those of badgers and foxes, so it's essential to discount those first.

Dog prints are most easily distinguished from fox prints by looking at the pattern they make as they walk. Dogs have usually been well fed at home, so when they're out for a walk it's all about socialising and checking out the lovely smells and other dogs' bottoms. Because of this a dog's trail is often circuitous as they wander about sniffing and exploring. Foxes, on the other hand, are less likely to muck about, unless they've

A red fox on the alert for prey.

already filled their tummies. They are usually more determined about where they are going and therefore leave much straighter trails.

| Fox footprint | Dog footprint | Cat footprint |

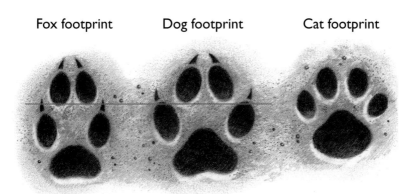

You can see from this illustration that placing a matchstick or other thin stick across the top of the front two toes gives you the final proof. On a fox track the stick should completely divide the print and not overlap the other two toes. Cats have retractable claws, so unless they're running or hunting you'll not see the claw marks at the front of their toes.

Dogs usually show all four feet in their trail, whereas a red fox often places the hind foot into the track of the front foot, creating a track that seems to have been made by a two-footed animal. Fox tracks are more compact, and you can sometimes see faint hair marks at the centre of a fox track. Occasionally a hair may be left in the track.

Bird song

Woodlands are the perfect place for spotting bird life and perhaps the most life-changing thing any naturalist can do is learn a few bird songs and calls. Songs are used to attract mates and defend territories. Calls are used to sound the alarm, beg for food, contact other individuals and so on.

Male blackbirds sing to defend their territory.

The best way of learning bird songs is through downloads on the web as well as from various apps, DVDs and CDs. Once you have some knowledge, you can try to identify the songs around you when you're outside.

TOP TIPS FOR A DEADLY DETECTIVE: Identifying blackbird calls

Blackbirds have a number of different calls that you can become familiar with.

Alarm call: a sort of scolding 'chink, chink, chink'. Look around and you may well see a domestic cat, the garden bird's worst enemy.

Startle call: similar, but often at a higher cadence when the animal is suddenly surprised.

Full song: the sound of the British countryside, a glorious fluted warble, sung from a high vantage point so as many other birds as possible will hear it. Especially common early in the morning when the air may be clearer, before noise pollution overwhelms the tune.

Subsong: a more half-hearted version of the song. This may be sung early in the season, or by an inexperienced bird. There is even a mournful version of subsong, which is sung if the bird has lost its young to a predator.

Contact calls: a way for birds to stay in touch with each other. Some birds such as long-tailed tits or goldcrests are continually chattering so the other members of the flock know where they are.

THE CASE OF:
THE TAWNY OWL

A few years back I decided to spend a night in the tallest tree in England, which is located in the grounds of a very beautiful public school. They kindly allowed me to put up ropes and climb into the very top branches, where I strung my hammock.

I then hauled up some food and a sleeping bag so I could spend the night there. Just to annoy me, the crew set up a barbecue below, and the smell of delicious food drifted to me while I ate boil-in-the-bag noodles!

I wanted to try and find some animals while I was up there, but when you're in a tree it's difficult to move around safely so I decided to bring the wildlife to me. When it was properly dark, I pulled out my tawny owl whistle. This is a carved piece of wood that you blow into to make the sound people associate with the UK's most common owl.

What most of us don't realise is that the 'twit twoo' of the tawny is actually from two owls. The first 'twit' or 'kewick' is a call, often marking out a home range. The second 'hooo' is more of a song, and from a different bird. Within minutes of starting to use my whistle, the resident tawny owl was frantically and indignantly calling, coming in to drive out what he thought was a challenger.

He flew right into the tree I was in!

I didn't use the whistle for long – you don't want to interrupt the bird's evening too much – but even lying there in my hammock, I got a great wildlife experience by having a little bit of wild know-how.

Eggs

If you find the remains of a bird's egg in a hedgerow, how do you know whether the occupant met a sticky end? Well, small eggs that have hatched, such as those of tits and thrushes, will be in two neat halves. The chick has used a temporary egg tooth on the end of its beak to chip around one end, then pushed its way out. Larger birds, such as swans and birds of prey, pierce holes and then expand their bodies, leaving several broken pieces.

In either case, the peck marks will come from the inside of the egg and the tough inner membrane will protrude from the inside out. Shells from such hatched eggs will rarely be near the nest, as parent birds remove them to avoid attracting predators.

Eggs taken by predators, on the other hand, are usually nearly whole, but with a single pecked

This egg probably hatched naturally.

This egg has been eaten by a predator.

Eggs attacked by predators

hole around the centre. The force has come from the outside, so the shell is folded in towards the centre. There may well be bits of yolk or white remaining in or on the shell.

Q. *What happened here?*
An artificial nest box on
a tree has had a circular
hole cut in it from the outside.
There is nesting material
inside, but no chicks or
eggs.

A. This is the work of the great spotted woodpecker. They are not after the eggs, but the young chicks, which they can hear moving around inside. Putting up a sheet of metal may deter them, although they have even been known to hammer through thin sheets of lead!

Feeding signs

It's common to find the remnants of various nuts, cones and seeds on the ground. Once you know what to look for, you can often tell exactly what's been feeding on them.

Hazelnut eaten
by small bird

• Tiny but neat holes in acorns are the work of a small passerine (perching bird) such as a great tit.
• Hazelnuts that are still attached to a branch but with irregular holes across them have been pecked open by woodpeckers.

These hazelnuts have been nibbled by dormice.

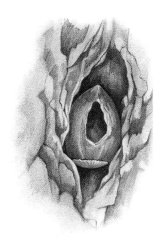

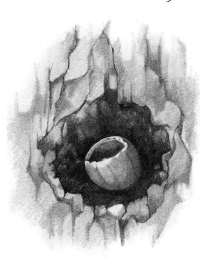

Hazelnut eaten
by woodpecker

Hazelnut eaten by nuthatch

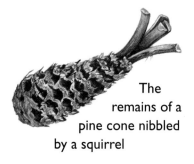

The remains of a pine cone nibbled by a squirrel

• Hazelnuts with their tops incredibly neatly removed have been nibbled open by dormice.
• A nut that has been completely split in two down its axis shows a squirrel has been at work.
• Nuts that have been jammed into gaps in bark, then hammered open, have probably been worked by a nuthatch.
• Pine cones that have been nibbled down to the base are also the work of squirrels.

The holes in this tree bark have been made by woodpeckers, and some also by solitary wasps.

Q. *what is this?*

A. If you find a pile of smashed up snail shells around a hard object such as a rock or hard tree root, this is inevitably the work of a song thrush. They pick up snails and batter them against a makeshift anvil to access the contents. Bank voles will not smash shells, but instead nibble down the spiral.

Q. *what created this spooky cobweb?*

A. The web has been spun by ermine moth caterpillars. They hide in the silk during the day and emerge to feed at night.

This is tinder fungus. When ground down, it's great for starting camp fires.

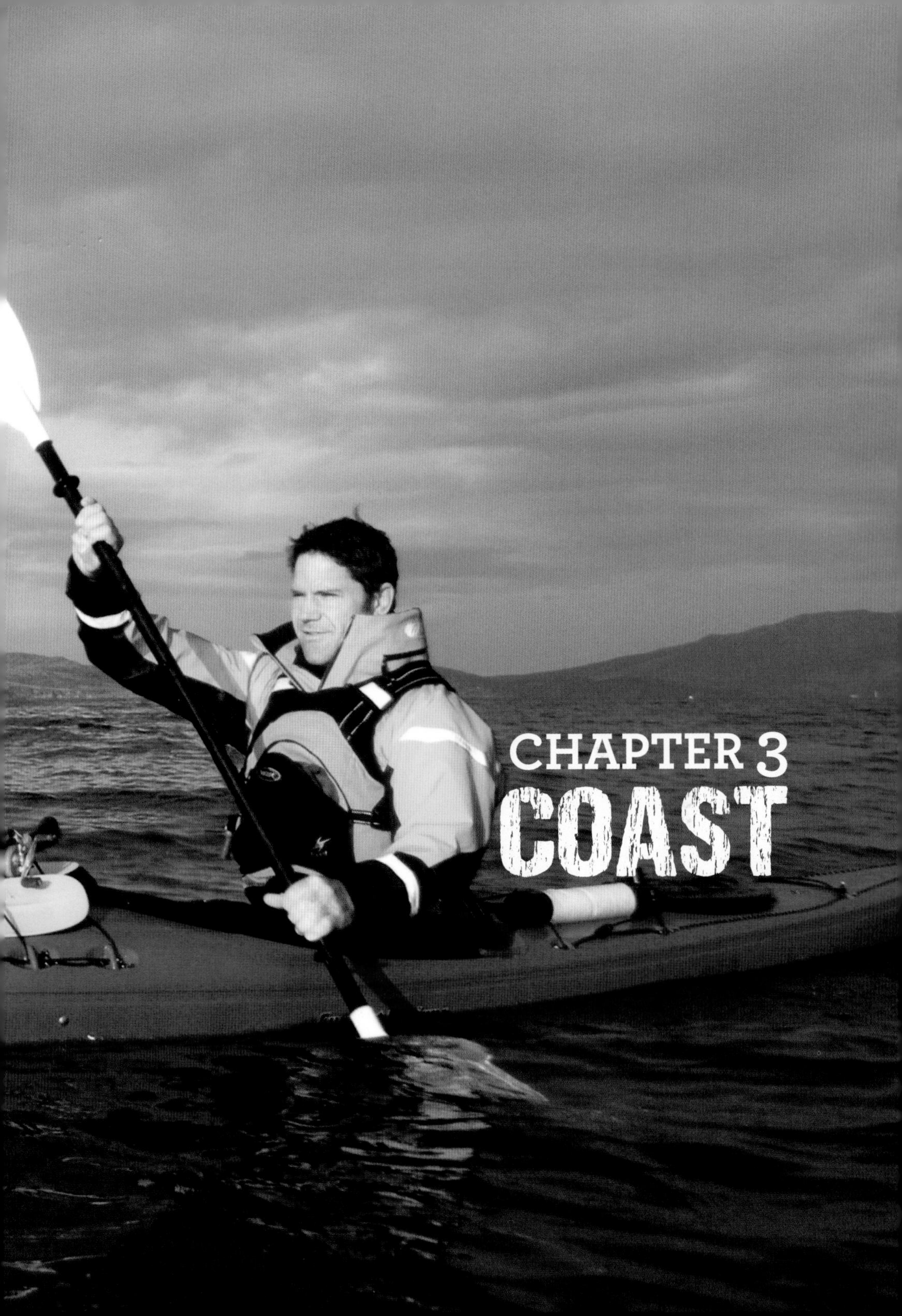

CHAPTER 3
COAST

If I fancy a day foraging, I head to the coast in search of mussels, scallops, limpets, seaweed and fresh fish. The twice-daily shift in the tides brings a bamboozlement of bounty for anyone who knows where to look. Of course, animals know this far better than we do, which makes the coast one of the best places to go looking for wildlife. Damp but not flooded sand is the perfect substrate for prints if you can keep ahead of the tides. Feeding signs are everywhere, so it's paradise for the seaside sleuth!

Exploring a rocky coastline in Scotland.

Never eat anything you find without checking with an adult and making absolutely sure it is safe. Some people are allergic to shellfish and these creatures can also include nasty stuff if they've been living in polluted waters.

Make sure you have a tide timetable if you're foraging along the coast so you don't get caught out. Watch out for the tides and the weather and never, ever go into the sea or out on a boat alone, or without someone with proper experience.

SEASHORE SIGNS

Sandy beaches are superb places to go searching for wild signs. As the tide ebbs, the damp sand that's left behind is awash with clues.

Gull footprint

Crab tracks

There are the casts left behind as various seashore worms dig down into their burrows. The lugworm is a large annelid worm, beloved of anglers, which leaves a very distinctive cast. They live in a U-shaped burrow. At the head is a saucer-shaped depression and at the base of the U is a twisty jumbled coil. Collecting lugworms for fishing requires a spade: they go deeper than you'll be able to dig with your hands – unless you're prepared to destroy your fingernails!

Wading birds will be searching for scrummy morsels such as lugworms. Curlews and possibly whimbrels are the only birds that have beaks long enough to delve this deep.

Lugworm cast on the sand.

65

Other birds, though, will leave behind little probing holes alongside their footprints.

Even more exciting and even more difficult to catch are razor shells, also known as razor clams because they look like old-fashioned cut-throat razors. These bivalve molluscs can only be uncovered at the very lowest tides.

Sea turtles leave distinctive marks in the sand when they travel up the beach to lay their eggs.

Razor clams have left these dimples in the sand.

THE CASE OF: THE WATER MONITOR

For me, Papua New Guinea has been one of the
most difficult but also most rewarding locations for an expedition.

On one trip, I found a set of crocodile tracks coming up
on to a sandy beach, making a circuit then returning to the water.
It didn't seem like the croc had stopped to bask, so I guessed that
she was coming ashore to guard a nearby nest.

With a couple of colleagues I set about exploring the
immediate area to find her nest. It proved quite easy,
as it had been partially excavated and there were the remnants
of leathery eggshells on the surface. My guess was that the
nest had been raided by a monitor lizard.

These tough, opportunistic lizards are some of the most
determined predators of crocodile nests, sensing them with their
long forked tongues, then digging into the ground with curved
talons that would look more at home on an eagle's feet. Not all
the crocodile's eggs had been taken and it seemed likely our culprit
would be back that night, so we set up a camera trap.

We returned the following morning and, as expected,
the nest had been destroyed, with all the eggs taken.

We couldn't wait to get back to camp to look through the images
and find out if my prediction had been correct. Sure enough,
there it was – a two-metre long water monitor lizard looking like
a dinosaur and licking its lips as it scoffed down crocodile eggs.
It was difficult not to feel sorry for the crocodile, whose efforts
had been wasted for another breeding season, but it was also
really satisfying to have used detective work to assess an
animal crime scene correctly.

Evidence of a crab's burrow.

Look out for dimples in the sand, possibly even with the mollusc's siphon poking through it. To coax them to the surface, pour some salty water into the hole, and the clam may come up, believing the tide has come in again.

Sea kayak

My favourite way to explore the coast is by sea kayak. It has the great advantage of allowing the adventurer to get to beaches that are utterly inaccessible to walkers or other kinds of boat.

I take to the water in a sea kayak.

Because sea kayaks have hatches in the front and back, you can take food and equipment for several weeks and be totally self-sufficient. They are also by far the best way to come across spectacular wildlife. On one especially memorable day, I paddled back from the Scilly Isles to the mainland, a ten-hour trip over open sea. On that one day we saw a host of spectacular birds including my first great shearwater, as well as common and bottlenose dolphins, porpoise, seals and sunfish. A minke whale and her calf came up among us, and a leatherback turtle swam into one of our kayaks; the first I'd seen in native waters. It was my best British wildlife day by far!

Be especially careful about watching the tides and weather, and never go to sea alone, or without a properly experienced person. Tides and weather conditions can change quickly and offshore winds can blow you farther out to sea than you want – and make it difficult to get back to the shore.

Q. *What made the holes in this mussel shell?*

A. This is a classic mark left behind by a predatory snail called a dog whelk. They bore through limpet or mussel shells using a tough lance called a radula.

Dog whelk

Q. *What are these?*

A. Lugworm casts and burrows.

Rockpools

Rockpools are tidal traps, superb for getting hands-on with wildlife. One of the simplest ways of getting to see what's

Sea anemones in a rockpool.

hiding inside is just to chuck in a little chunk of smelly food – perhaps the cheese from your sandwich, or a piece of tuna. Then sit back, making sure you keep a low profile so that fish and other animals inside won't be able to see you. Pretty soon the pool will come alive, as shrimp, crabs and small fish come out to investigate and get stuck in!

Dunes

In some areas sand dunes form at the back of beaches, where onshore winds drive beach sands into carved hillocks often held together by a matrix of hardy grasses. Lots of wildlife uses

Ruby-tailed wasp.

Sand digger wasps.

these environments: birds nest in them, foxes hunt and scavenge there. Some of our most colourful mini-beasts are also found here. The ruby-tailed wasp and the male sand lizard in his vibrant green breeding colours are two of the southern UK's most exotic sights.

Sand lizard.

Q. *What made this track in the sand?*

A. This was made by a female elephant seal who had dragged herself way up into the sand dunes to give birth. Elephant seals are the largest of all seals, with male southern elephant seals weighing almost as much as an actual elephant!

A baby grey seal in the dunes.

///// THE CASE OF: /////
THE SAILFISH

The fastest fish in the sea is also one of the most difficult to find.

If I want to find thresher sharks, I'll go to a seamount
where they come up early in the morning to be given
a grooming by smaller fish called cleaner wrasse.

If I want to swim with great whites, I'll go to somewhere like
Australia, South Africa or Mexico where they're known to occur,
and fill the water with stinky fish blood to attract them.

Sailfish, however, cannot be tempted to come to you,
and could be anywhere in the deep blue. They're lightning-quick
inhabitants of the open sea and, without some detective work,
they are almost impossible to find.

We went out in a boat off the eastern coast of Mexico,
searching not for the sailfish themselves, nor even for the bait fish
they feed on, but for the frigate birds that feed on those bait fish.
At the end of a long, hard first day at sea, we had seen nothing
and were ready to give up and head for home. Just as I'd done a
deflated final piece to camera, I noticed what looked like a swarm
of bees way off on the horizon. I shouted to the boat captain,
who exploded with excitement and slammed the boat into top
speed. When we got close, we could see the swarm was actually
hundreds of frigate birds swooping down to the surface to
grab foot-sized sardines grouped in a tightly packed defensive
formation known as a bait ball. Slicing the surface were the fins
of our sailfish, feeding on the small fish from below.

We dived in and spent nearly an hour with the fastest fish
in the sea zipping about our ears – a truly unforgettable encounter,
made possible by a bit of Deadly Detecting!

CHAPTER 4
FRESH WATER

Clean water is one of the most important things that living organisms require, so freshwater environments are oases for life. Rivers, lakes and streams are the mainstay of any Deadly Detective looking for a wild encounter. Along their banks, you may find the tracks and signs of the terrestrial creatures that have come to drink or perhaps to hunt like the previous picture of me finding croc tracks. Under the water you can find a baffling array of both vertebrate and invertebrate life.

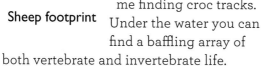

Sheep footprint

Heron footprint

The animals you find will change throughout the year. In spring and summer, a local pond may be home to nesting coots,

Heron tracks in the sand.

grebes and herons. Dragonflies and damselflies may flit over the surface, and grass snakes and frogs will be frequent visitors. In winter most of these will disappear, to be replaced by thousands of migrating ducks and geese arriving from the far north to take advantage of what to them are balmy climes.

Gull footprint

Waterside prints

Soft mud or sand at the edges of rivers are some of the best places to look for tracks. When you're by a river, look for the place where you would cross – the place where it's narrowest, where the water is shallow or the flow least powerful. Many animals will also choose these easier crossing points.

By the way, wading into a river is an excellent idea for anyone who wants to lose a tracker. Footprints are washed away in the water and the person's scent is carried downstream – sniffer dogs can't follow and the trail is lost.

Q. *what is this?*

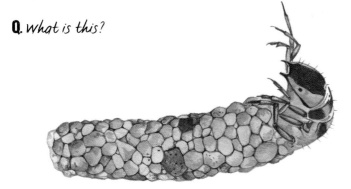

A. Flying insects called caddisflies have a stage of their life cycle where they live underwater as larvae. They gather together bits of twig and stone and weave them together in silk to make a protective sleeping bag to keep them safe from predatory fish that would like to munch them up.

Searching for dragonfly and caddisfly larvae in a freshwater pond.

Swan mussels

These bivalve molluscs live in the bottom of rivers, and are filter feeders. They have a remarkable life cycle. Each spring they produce parasitic larvae that float up into the water

Swan mussel

and attach themselves to fish, feeding off mucus (a slippery substance that covers the body of their host). Within a few weeks, though, the larvae drop off the fish and grow into adult mussels. Look in the sediment in the bottom of ponds and rivers for trails resembling shallow continuous trenches that look as if they could have been made by a human thumb. These are the marks made by the super-slow-moving mussels as they trawl around the bottom.

Otters

Otters are large members of the weasel or mustelid family. Look out for an otter den, called a holt, in rocky banks or reed beds, typically with the entrance dug into the roots of a riverbank tree. Inland freshwater otters spend the day inside the holt and only emerge at night to feed. Otters living on the coast, in areas such as Scotland, rely on the bounty brought in twice a day by the tides, and they are much more likely to be active in full daylight.

Otters will often cut corners when travelling upstream, so look for trails that cut across the corner of a meandering stream then head back into the water. When travelling downstream otters stay in the water and use the stream to power them along. When moving fast on land, they use the classic weasel bounding movement and their tracks may show four quite tightly grouped prints; tail marks may also be evident. Five digital pads usually show in both front and rear tracks, and you can often see the webbing between the toes, used to assist in the otter's swimming.

An otter leaves its black slimy droppings (called spraint) on quite obvious landmarks. These are a signpost to other animals, letting them know that the otter is around, is looking for a mate, or that perhaps this patch is his and competitors should keep moving. The smell of otter spraint has been described as being like wet hay or jasmine tea! A spraint

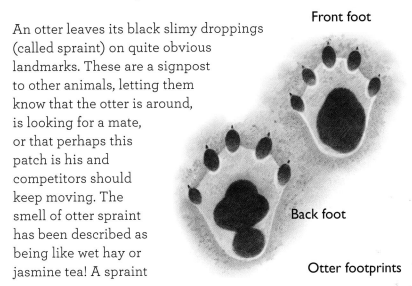

Front foot

Back foot

Otter footprints

An otter and her young.

keeps its smell for ages and may contain evident chunks of fish scales, crayfish shell and feathers from birds (moorhens are a real favourite). When they have been feeding on fish, otters will often eat the head first and leave the tail. Otters living at the coast also create scrapes of fresh water where they can groom through their coats.

A shed snake skin.

Many snakes, particularly large ones, live in or near water as they can move easily through the stream and it supports their bulk. Discarded (sloughed or shed) skins are a great sign that snakes are at large!

THE BLACK CAIMAN

When filming giant river otters in Peru, we also wanted to try to get some footage of the giant black caiman (a kind of crocodile) that was rumoured to live in the lake. I managed to catch some small caimans at night, but nothing like the monster we had been told lived there.

Deadly director Giles decided to try using a camera trap, so we found an area at the side of the lake where there were evident drag marks from a large animal going into and out of the water. We got a piece of stinking meat and pulled it over the ground and into the water so any passing croc would get a whiff, and set up the trap with a tripwire. Anything that stumbled through or over the wire would trigger the camera.

When we came back next morning, the meat lure was gone, but it seemed the camera had malfunctioned. There was hours of footage on the camera, but it just showed blank background, with no animals at all. It had been a total failure. I'd nearly finished going through the footage when I screamed in excitement. With no more than two minutes left to go on the tape, our monster caiman appeared in glorious detail, exiting the water and scoffing down the meat before returning to the depths. It was all incredibly creepy, and a triumph for our detective work!

CHAPTER 5
TEMPERATE FOREST

The biggest woodlands in the world are not tropical jungles such as the Amazon, but the vast forests in the far north of the northern hemisphere, known as the boreal and taiga. These are covered in snow for much of the year, then plagued by pesky biting flies when it's warmer! They can be ferociously uncomfortable and challenging, but they contain some of the last great wilderness on our planet, making them a must for any adventurer. In these forests, knowing nature's signs can keep you alive, preventing you from wandering into a grizzly bear with her young, or helping you know when you're being stalked by a Siberian tiger.

In winter, when thick snow carpets the taiga, much is hidden and buried. Small mammals live their days in tunnels beneath the crust; others turn white and vanish into the background. However, as the wildlife gets harder to see, it becomes far easier to track, its memory left behind in the snow. Look out for lots of different kinds of birds. Most bears will be tucked away in hibernation, but you can spot the tracks of birds, cats, rabbits and hares with ease.

Bird droppings

Birds only have one exit for their bodily waste, so bird droppings are usually undigested food remains mixed with urine. They often take on the form of a white paste. These droppings can be tremendously important in helping you to identify bird roosts and nests. If you find a patch of ground spattered with white, look up – there may be a nesting site in the trees overhead.

Small birds usually have well-formed droppings that might contain seed or fruit fragments. Plant eaters, such as geese and swans, produce cylindrical green and white droppings that contain some fibrous matter. Carnivorous species tend to

Aerial view of the taiga in the northern hemisphere.

lift their tails and power-squirt white goo. They're particularly likely to do this just before taking flight – effectively lightening their load!

Bird pellets

Bird pellets are not actually poo, though it is quite easy to mistake them for mammal droppings. They are the indigestible parts of prey which the bird regurgitates and coughs up through its beak. Owls are particularly in need of this solution, as they generally swallow their prey in a single gulp, but many other birds also produce pellets.

A closer look at some owl pellets.

Looking at pellets is a superb way of finding out what a bird has been eating. You can find info in books or on the internet that helps you figure out whether the jawbone you've discovered inside a pellet is from a vole, a shrew, a mouse, fish,

frog or another bird. Their position may also give away a well-used perching post where the bird returns to devour its prey or keep watch over its hunting grounds. One way of telling pellets from poo is that pellets do not have a twisted end – fox droppings, among others, often do.

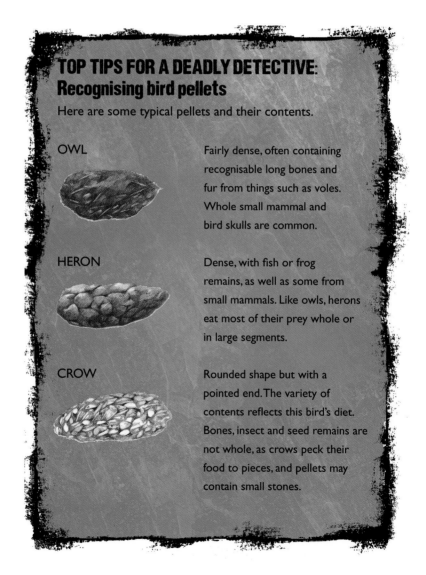

TOP TIPS FOR A DEADLY DETECTIVE: Recognising bird pellets

Here are some typical pellets and their contents.

OWL

Fairly dense, often containing recognisable long bones and fur from things such as voles. Whole small mammal and bird skulls are common.

HERON

Dense, with fish or frog remains, as well as some from small mammals. Like owls, herons eat most of their prey whole or in large segments.

CROW

Rounded shape but with a pointed end. The variety of contents reflects this bird's diet. Bones, insect and seed remains are not whole, as crows peck their food to pieces, and pellets may contain small stones.

VULTURE, HAWK, EAGLE Pellets contain only small bone fragments, as prey tends to be too large to be swallowed intact. May contain lots of rodent fur.

FALCON May contain fur and feathers. Those of raptors such as hobbies, which catch dragonflies on the wing, may contain invertebrate remains. Kestrel pellets (left) always contain vole fragments.

GULL These pellets contain a real hodgepodge of scavenged food and prey. There may well be indigestible bits of plastic and other garbage in their pellets too – a sign of how these animals have adapted to human society.

FEATHERS

Usually it's the tail or flight feathers of birds that offer the best chances for identification. Good field guides can allow you to pinpoint the species from one single feather.

Moulted feathers

Once a feather has grown, it is effectively dead. Over time, the keratin, the material it is made of, starts to degenerate and become brittle. By the end of the breeding season, most flight feathers will have worn out and need to be replaced. Most birds moult annually so their plumage is in peak condition in readiness for the winter, particularly if they are going to migrate or spend the winter in cold climes.

Some birds, such as ducks and geese, replace all these flight feathers in one go, leaving a period of time when they cannot fly or only fly poorly. During this time they will often take on duller colours in order to be less obvious to predators. This is known as 'eclipse'. Check out the mallards at your local pond in the summer; there'll be no flashy green heads on the males, as they are not trying to impress the lady ducks! Moulted feathers are usually found individually, complete from the very base of the shaft with both quill and plume intact, and may be in poor condition.

Victim of a bird of prey

The feather will have been plucked out whole, but the quill may show beak marks from the aggressor. Birds of prey often decapitate their catches first, as the brains are particularly prized as food, but they leave behind the legs and wings.

Sparrowhawks make an incredible mess of their prey, hitting it with huge force, then tearing its feathers out at the root. I've seen a female sparrowhawk hit a wood pigeon midair, killing it instantly, then crash down into a suburban garden with her victim. The pigeon was much bigger than the raptor, but the sparrowhawk had clearly decided the middle of the lawn was too public a place to eat her meal. She grabbed the dead pigeon with a single talon and flew with it into a nearby chunk of pampas grass, where she tore out all its feathers before feasting on its

A bald eagle feeding on an American coot. These birds often thieve food off other predators, including other bald eagles!

brains! If you come upon a circular pile of feathers on your lawn, with the head and breast muscles eaten, it may well be the remains of a bird that has met a sticky end at the talons of a sparrowhawk.

Victim of a small mammal predator

Stoats and other members of the weasel family often drag the bird away whole and hide or bury it. Any separate feathers you find will have been bitten off rather than plucked – most of the quill will be missing, and there may be saliva near the bite mark.

Victim of a medium-sized mammal predator

Foxes pull a bird's feathers out in mouthfuls, leaving the plumes

Remains of a bird killed by a mammal.

and quills mauled. Down feathers may be soggy and matted with spit as you can see to the left. Foxes also cache (hide) their prey.

Victim of large mammal or reptile predator
The killer may not bother plucking the feathers off the bird before eating it. There may be blood and a few remnant feathers spread at the kill site.

Q. *What happened here?*

A. This shrew has been caught by a predator, which may have mistaken it for a vole or mouse. Shrews have special glands on their sides which make them taste bad so most predators won't eat them – except barn owls, which seem to love them!

Q: *What left these footprints?*

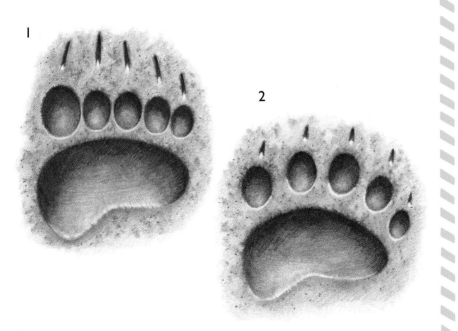

1

2

A. 1 Grizzly bear. 2 Black bear.

What to do if you meet a bear

An encounter with a bear is one of the most special, most memorable moments any naturalist will ever have. Watching grizzlies catching salmon from a waterfall, or a black bear munching grasses like a big carnivore cow is unforgettable. Strictly speaking, though, all bears are carnivores and have the capacity to do great harm or even kill a human being. Here are some guidelines for how to act if you unexpectedly come across one in the wild.

Encountering bears in the summer when food such as salmon is plentiful is usually safe. However, bears can be very different animals in early spring when they have just come out of hibernation and are effectively starving. If you are out hiking at this time of year, you must stay even more vigilant than normal. Mothers with young cubs can also be fiercely protective and should be avoided. Any bear that is injured, feels threatened or cornered, or is on a kill can be very dangerous indeed.

Taking care around your campsite is essential. Cook and keep food away from where you sleep. Don't even keep toothpaste in your tent, as bears will smell it from a mile away.

Standing up like this doesn't always mean that a grizzly bear is ready to attack. They sometimes stand on their hind legs to get a better view of their surroundings.

THE CASE OF: THE GRIZZLY BEAR

The largest land predator is the brown bear (specifically the brown bears that live on Kodiak Island off North America's west coast). If one stood up in your front room, it would bang its head on your ceiling, and these bears can weigh as much as a horse! This gives a Detective certain benefits when tracking them. As grizzlies are so heavy, they will leave tracks in all kinds of ground and some are so deep that they stay in place for days on end.

On a sea kayaking expedition in Alaska, I woke in the morning and looked outside to see a perfectly fresh set of bear tracks going right past my tent. We followed the trail very carefully – it's really important not to surprise bears, especially when they're feeding. Many Alaskans wear a bell on their rucksacks, or routinely shout out 'Hey bear!' as they walk, so bears know they're coming. Eventually we came to a waterfall, and splashing in the water fishing for salmon was not one but three bears. They all looked big enough to be adults, but on closer inspection we saw one was clearly a mature female and the other two were her grown-up male young. They were obviously about two years old and she kept chasing them off, telling them to leave her alone and take care of themselves.

Eventually one of the males decided to go it alone and he wandered in our direction. It was only then that we realised that the tide had come in and the water level had come up, cutting us off. In order to get out, the bear would have to walk right over the top of us! He only saw us when we were way too close to do anything other than stand our ground. It was a really frightening moment as he stopped and sniffed the air, obviously deciding what to do next. He may have only been two, but he was huge and could easily have killed all of us if he had wanted to. After a few tense minutes, he retraced his steps, walking all the way back over the waterfall to avoid us. Lesson learned!

CHAPTER 6
MOUNTAINS

*Heading through the icefall section of the Cholatse glacier,
one of the most dangerous parts of any mountain.*

Mountains are my favourite environment on Earth – they are
phenomenally challenging places where all true adventurers
feel at home! An alpine meadow in summer is bursting with
life such as wildflowers, orchids, butterflies and birds. In winter
only the hardiest remain, but with snow on the ground this
is prime time for the tracker who can read the comings and
goings of invisible creatures by the stories they leave behind
in the white stuff.

Mountains are a challenging environment for wildlife too, but
there are creatures that are well-adapted to these surroundings
such as pika, ibex and marmot.

Pika

Pika and track.

These small,
curious
animals
look like
big-eared
mice, but
are actually
lagomorphs (members of
the rabbit family). They
are adapted to life at high
altitude and they store
plants, including piles of
flowers, in their burrows
as food stores to last them
through the coldest winter
months. They have a
hopping gait and their footprints are distinctly rabbit-like, with
much larger hind feet.

They urinate on prominent rocks and the urine dries to a white messy stain – another sign to watch for. Their scat is spherical and very much like rabbit pellets. Pika also ingest their poo to gain the most from its nutrients.

During the winter, pika scrape aside snow in order to reach the grasses, moss and lichen beneath. Over these areas will also be their droppings, which are collections of small pellets, clumped together.

Ibex

These goat-antelopes, or caprids, are true mountain dwellers and dance about the slopes on their small but insanely grippy hooves. The females and younger animals tend to stick together while mature males spend most of the year away from these groups. These males use their long, curved horns to battle with competitors. Males have beards, females do not. You may see prints of their cloven hooves and these usually show a walking gait. The scat is in the form of pellets, but may be together in a lump.

Young ibex.

Marmot

These creatures, which look like oversized hamsters, are incredibly endearing, very social and real mountain specialists. In the Himalayas I've sat for hours watching the males wrestling with each other, seeming to take themselves incredibly seriously until they tumble over in comical fashion. You need to take care in areas where they have made burrow systems.

A marmot pops up from its burrow.

I know a few mountaineers who've gone through the ground up to their knees – a very good way to sprain or break an ankle. The burrow complex will usually be on a south-facing slope, and the marmots may use natural holes in rocks and rubble for their entrances.

Camp toilet!

The 'long drop' is the camp toilet of choice. It must be as deep as you can bear to dig and should be filled in when you move on. Even seemingly huge areas like a high mountain base camp can become polluted very quickly if you don't make a dedicated facility. Making a toilet when you're in remote environments is absolutely critical. Human poo contains all kinds of nasty toxins that can make you very ill, so you have to be incredibly careful. If you're camping on a river, the toilet must be downstream of camp so you don't contaminate your water source. Then always gather drinking water, wash plates and so on upstream of it. If you don't make a dedicated toilet, take a shovel, dig a shallow hole and poo into it. Then burn your toilet paper, and make doubly sure to wash and disinfect your hands!

///// ■ THE CASE OF: /////

THE SNOW LEOPARD

The team and I had trekked five days up into the high alpine pastures of Bhutan, a tiny country in the Himalayas between India and China. We'd gone up to more than 5,000 metres, well above the tree line, looking for signs of tiger.

We were pretty confident we'd find nothing. As we approached the highest meadows, we saw five or six vultures circling an area of the mountainside. We watched for a while; perhaps they were merely all riding the same thermal air current and would soon be gone – but no, they were surely circling over a carcass – vulture food!

At the pasture we met a yak herder who lived there with his family and yaks. I asked him some questions, including, 'Do you ever see any big cats up here?' and fully expected him to say no. Instead he replied, 'I see snow leopard here all the time. One took one of my yaks two days ago.' I was flabbergasted. Snow leopard are among the most elusive and rare animals in the world, and I had thought I would go my whole career without seeing one in the wild. This I had to check out.

I went up on the slopes where the kill had happened, and there, clear as day, were several lines of prints from a female snow leopard. That night I was lying in my tent when I heard the yak herder's dogs going crazy, barking fit to burst. Something was out there, a predator that was a threat to the yaks. With my heart banging in my chest, I grabbed my small camera, which had a night-time shooting feature, and went out into the darkness. Heading towards the noise, I found a line of prints, so fresh that they were still filling up with water, with little grains of dust circulating

inside them. They had been made minutes before. The snow leopard could have been out there in the darkness watching me.

Next day, we found out that the leopard had killed a blue sheep on the slopes above camp. The sheep carcass looked as if it had been sawn in half. The front part remained and, even more intriguing, around the corpse were much larger prints – from a male snow leopard. In this one valley, a male and female were hunting together. This meant they were mating or had young cubs to feed. There was little doubt in my mind that they would be back that night to finish off the blue sheep. The only problem was that I had no camera traps with me and no proper night-time filming equipment. The infrared feature on my little camera worked, but I would have to be really close. The only option was to sit mere metres away from the carcass, on my own, and see what happened. The rest of the crew thought I was insane.

Snow leopard footprint.

That night I sat in total silence and darkness for four hours. Then by my shoulder a chilling snarl cut through to my bones. The snow leopard was right at my back. He had crept in without seeing me, and probably smelled me at the last minute. He could have leapt on me and torn me apart, but he sprinted off up the hillside, scattering tiny pebbles down around me.

Next morning I went back to look at the prints. They clearly showed claws out to give him grip as he sprinted away. I may well have got closer than any other human being to a truly wild snow leopard, and even though I didn't see him, it remains one of my finest wildlife encounters.

A snow leopard on the prowl.

TOP TIPS FOR A DEADLY DETECTIVE:
Building a snow cave

The most important strategy for survival at night in the polar conditions of high mountains is getting out of the wind into a space that can be warmed, even if only by your own body heat. A snow hole is usually really uncomfy. However, this is a million times better than spending a night in the open!

First, select your spot. A corniced ridge is ideal, or a snowdrift with a steep side. The snow needs to be compact and hopefully not still drifting.

Make sure you are well wrapped up. Your gloves will certainly get very wet unless you happen to have a pair of rubber gloves over the top! A saw and snow shovel are the best tools for the job, but a cooking pot, snow shoes, ski, broken branch or even your hands may have to do.

Begin tunnelling in. This first tunnel needs to be head height and a body length in depth. Now start another tunnel alongside it. This tunnel must be parallel to the first, and of a similar length and depth.

Link the two tunnels together, forming a flat area that will be your bed. This must be raised up from the floor. Make the ceiling as low as you can bear, as a smaller area is easier to keep warm. Try to keep this ceiling as smooth as possible. As the area warms, snow will melt and if you have any irregularities, drips will concentrate there and splitter splatter on your face!

Fill in the entrance to one of the tunnels and half fill in the other, then use your pack to create a door to keep out the wind. If you are using a stove inside, make sure you dig a hole in the ceiling to allow carbon monoxide to escape.

Be warned, snow caves can collapse, which makes them very dangerous indeed. Only do this with the help of an expert.

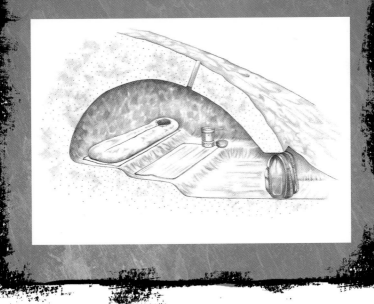

THE CLOUDED LEOPARD

Golden langur.

In Bhutan, where the lowlands start to soar into the mighty Himalayas, the Lost Lands team was searching for evidence of Bengal tigers. With cameraman Graham and soundie Nick, I'd been walking the trails around base camp for three weeks, gathering footprints and poo from the animals that were obviously around. We rarely saw any actual animals, though, apart from the endangered golden langur monkeys that chattered from the treetops and almost seemed to be laughing at our failure!

Towards the end of the trip, we'd all really got our eyes in and were spotting tracks from the smaller cat species every day, as well as very occasional signs from the tiger we so badly wanted to document. The team were walking down a riverbed when we came across a thin fallen tree that had dropped down to about chest height. In the centre of it was a dropping as thin as my thumb, dark, with a few small pieces of feather in it. The tree was too light to support the weight of a leopard and the scat was too small for even a young animal. It needed to be from a cat with superb climbing ability which would take birds even in the forest canopy. I was so certain of what had left these signs that it was as if the animal was standing on the branch in front of me. It had to be a clouded leopard.

We set up some camera traps to try to find out if my hunch had been correct. A few days later, our cat specialist, Kashmira Kakati, called me into the edit suite tent where all of the footage from our many camera traps was being collated. She seemed really excited

and I soon realised why. The trap we'd set out in our riverbed
had recorded a wonderful shot of my clouded leopard. And that was
not all. You could clearly see an enlarged teat and a swollen belly and
Kashmira told me in no uncertain terms that the leopard was pregnant!
So not only had we gained evidence of a rarely seen cat,
but also the knowledge that this one was about to have cubs —
part of a happy future for the species in the area.
Wonderful stuff.

The long drop

Anyone who goes on expeditions for a living soon racks up a fair amount of terrible toilet stories. When I did my Himalayan expedition training with the Indian army, the entire team had to go out together after breakfast and dig a long trench. Then we'd all squat in a line together, passing the toilet roll and talking about last night's sleep! However, being as we were in the most magnificent place on Earth, it was a regular 'poo with a view'!

Nothing is as frustrating as waking in the middle of the night up high and realising that you need to go. You're tucked up so warm in your sleeping bag, and outside might be –30 degrees and blowing a gale! On one Himalayan trip, though, I went outside and noticed a crisp slice taken out of the full moon, growing by the minute. It was a perfect lunar eclipse that I'd have totally missed if it hadn't been for needing the high-altitude bathroom.

In Guyana, we inadvertently built our toilet next to the burrow of a big tarantula and so had to make a sign pointing down to it to make sure no one trod on it while going to the loo in the night! Probably most horrid of all was at base camp in New Guinea. After we'd been there for a month, we had torrential rains which flushed all the maggots out of the long drop. Within a day, our camp was plagued by flies and eventually had to be evacuated. Yuck!

If your camp is constantly moving, then don't bother digging a long drop. Instead just dig a hole as a sort of porta-potty and cover it afterwards. Excess toilet paper should be burned, or if you are feeling really tough, use natural material like moss.

The toilet with the most magnificent view on Earth.

CHAPTER 7
ARCTIC CIRCLE

Very cold Arctic environments are a mixed blessing for the tracker. There's little life, particularly at the coldest times of year – more species of insects could be found in one old English oak than in the entire Arctic Circle. You can go for long periods of time with spotting any signs. High winds and snow can obliterate tracks within minutes, so a trail can quickly go cold – quite literally! However, if conditions are right, nothing holds a track better than crisp snow. And nothing beats the excitement of coming across the enormous paw prints of a polar bear or the trails of a pack of grey wolves. These are moments that make all the hours spent in study worthwhile.

Arctic fox

These foxes have disproportionately small ears and legs. This reduces the surface area of their extremities, therefore leaving less of themselves to get chilled by Arctic winds. They are

An Arctic fox.

greyish-brown in the summer and pure white in the winter. The undersides of their feet are clad in hair to keep them insulated, so their prints look furry in the snow. Their track is small for a canid (member of the dog family), and the claws do not always show. Their scat has a tapered end and is mostly composed of undigested parts of mammal and bird prey. These foxes follow polar bears to scavenge their kills, so it's quite common to see huge bear prints with smaller fox tracks alongside. Other signs include scrapes they spend the daytime in, and dens burrowed into the ground.

Wolf

Their track is about the size of a cricket ball, or even larger in the biggest males. Their front paws are larger than the rear ones, with claws usually evident, and registration (foot in foot) is common. However, this may involve not only the

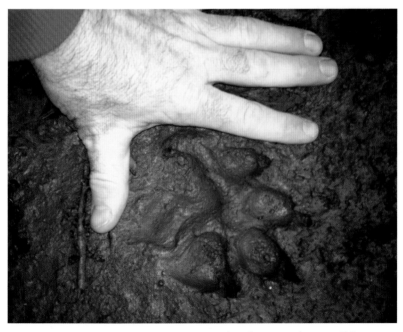

My hand compared to a wolf footprint.

A grey wolf.

feet of one individual; the whole pack may walk in the same footprints. This saves an enormous amount of energy in snow for the wolves as the first animal will compress the snow so the others won't have to wade through the deep stuff, but it can make it very difficult to figure out how many animals you are tracking! The scat is usually pure black, with a consistency like toothpaste. The tips are tapered and usually contain hair and bone fragments.

Other wolf signs

The alpha wolf marks its territory using urine as the pack travels. These scent marks are usually left on raised objects such as tree stumps and boulders and there may also be scratch marks alongside. Early in the year the female's urine may contain blood, which indicates she is ready to mate.

Lynx

A lynx's feet are huge for its body size and this makes its tracks easy to identify. Its feet act like snowshoes to keep the animal up off thick snow. As lynx are solitary, they can't take advantage of the footprints of other lynx, so even though they're a quarter of the weight of a wolf, their track is a similar size. The track can be quite indistinct, as there is so much hair insulating the footpads. Lynx tend to stick to forest edges where they can track their favourite food, the snowshoe hare.

The lynx's large furry feet help it move easily on the snow.

You might also spot other signs of lynx. Adults may urinate more than 20 times in every mile, leaving a smelly trail through the snow. Their scat differs from that of canids in being blunt-ended, with constrictions throughout it. You may also notice places on trees where lynx have rubbed their cheeks and taken off some of the bark. Lynx make dens where they give birth, usually inside hollow logs.

A lynx resting.

Q. *What do you think has happened in this photo?*

A. A coyote has crept up on a duck in the snow. At the last minute, as the coyote lunged forward, the duck took flight. The angel-like marks in the snow are from the duck's flight feathers as it brushed the ground. From the lack of blood or feathers, this one clearly got away.

Polar bear

On average the polar bear is the largest land carnivore, though individual Kodiak brown bears can be larger. The polar bear's footprint is truly unmistakable. It's huge, showing five toes on both front and rear feet, and there is dense hair on the underside which keeps the tootsies warm – you can sometimes see this in the print! Polar bears have a nonchalant ambling gait, with the toes

Polar bear footprint

turned inwards, and their tracks occur in pairs. If a bear breaks into a run or launches an attack, their prints are much more spread out and very deep; snow will be smashed everywhere.

Polar bears rely on sea ice to hunt. As the ice breaks up in the summer, they may head to dry land, go farther north in search of thicker ice, or end up stranded on ice floes far from land. These bears may swim 100 kilometres or more to get to a better spot. Scent is much more important to animals in the Arctic than anywhere else. The air is so clean, and has so few odours, that polar bears have been observed walking towards a seal

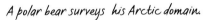

A polar bear surveys his Arctic domain.

Polar bear tracks on an ice floe.

carcass they must have detected through scent from as much as 30 kilometres away.

A sure sign of a polar bear kill is a massive amount of blood staining the snow. Quite often the bear only eats the blubber off a seal, walrus or whale carcass, wasting what we would consider the good bit, and may return to large prey over and again.

If you find a carcass with polar bear signs around it, leave the area immediately, and DO NOT camp anywhere nearby. In fact, even if you camp 10 or 20 miles away from the carcass, you should ensure you have someone on guard duty at all times. A camp in polar bear territory should also be surrounded with a detection system, such as trip wires. These can be connected to flares that ignite if the wire is tripped. Because food is so scarce in polar regions and there is no vegetable matter on the pack ice, polar bears see anything that walks as a potential meal. They are pretty much the only animals that will, in most circumstances, hunt down human beings, and they'll follow them for long distances in order to launch an attack. Perhaps no other animal on Earth demands such vigilance.

Other signs of a polar bear include its scat, which is really big, about the size of a Christmas cracker, and laden with bits of seal – undigested remains! In the summer, scat may contain berries, kelp or vegetation. I even found some filled with the plastic remains of a trainer insole!

Walrus

Walrus are very curious animals – they are seals that can reach nearly two tonnes in weight and can have tusks as long as my leg. Their scientific name means 'walks on their teeth', and they do use their massive tusks to draw themselves up on to the ice. Gouge marks on ice floes are a sure sign that walrus have been resting there. On beaches where walrus regularly haul out you may find scores of shells of bivalves such as clams that are completely intact. The mollusc has simply been sucked out of its shell by a walrus.

A walrus on an ice floe.

Ermine

A member of the mustelid (weasel) family, the ermine or stoat is a really remarkable animal. In cold parts of the world, it grows a nice white coat in winter which provides perfect camouflage against the snow. It has a classic mustelid print,

TOP TIPS FOR A DEADLY DETECTIVE:
Know your ice

Icebergs are vast chunks of ancient ice that have fallen off or 'calved' from glaciers. They can be the size of skyscrapers, are made of dense ice that may be thousands of years old and thus don't melt for a long time.

Pack ice is frozen sea. As seawater is salty, it will not freeze till below freezing point.

White ice is usually safe to walk on, but grey is not so thick and should be treated with care.

Black ice can be paper thin and must be avoided.

Pancake ice forms as small patches of sea freeze, then blows around in the wind forming circular crusts. This is very difficult to drag a sled over. All sea ice is active and mobile, so will move around with currents, tides and wind and is potentially very dangerous terrain.

Shore ice forms from frozen sea at the boundary of land and ocean. It may last longer than the floating ice.

Ermine footprint

with five evident toes on each foot, though the little toe may not show. The interdigital pad is arrow-shaped.

The classic gait is a bounding gallop, typical of the weasel family, and trails will show clusters of foot tracks close together. Ermine rarely run in a dead straight line for long, and their hyperactive nature is expressed in the twists and turns of their trails. If an ermine is dragging prey such as a rabbit that is much larger than itself, there will be evident drag marks to one side of the trail. Scat is often deposited in obvious high places as an advertisement. It's long and thin, folds back on itself and has tapered ends.

Ermine scat

Wolverine

The heaviest member of the weasel family, the wolverine still has tracks, trails and scats that are noticeably mustelid.

A wolverine tracks its prey.

Their track can show all five toes with claws, although – as with the ermine – the little toe may not appear. The interdigital pad is arrow-shaped. Their gallop is slightly offset, and their tracks are not as closely grouped as in other species.

Wolverines readily travel on already packed trails and roads for ease. As they're very low-slung and quite heavy animals, wolverines may well rub their stomach over stumps protruding from the snow, so look out for traces of hair. Their scat is a long

135

cord, doubled back on itself and with tapered ends. It contains hair from prey and scavenged food. Wolverines may bury carcasses and return to them and dig very powerfully.

Snowy environment – rabbits and hares

Tracks of these animals are some of the most frequently seen in snowy environments, and if you're looking at them, you can guarantee that predators are as well! Typically, you'll see trails that have been created by the animal's small fore feet being placed close together and then the much larger rear feet coming to either side and in front. Sometimes rabbits and hares make seemingly aimless circles, presumably in order to throw predators off their trail.

Rabbit footprint

Trail of a snowshoe hare.

A snowshoe hare.

Rabbit droppings

Other signs include plants protruding through the snow that have had their tips chewed off. Rabbits and hares may strip trees of bark, but only to a very low height. In extremely lean times, they've even been known to feed on the carcasses of dead animals! The other slightly yucky thing that rabbits do is to eat their own poo in order to get the maximum nutriment out of it. Also look out for hare forms – flattened areas on the ground where they sleep during the day, perhaps under conifer branches.

Musk oxen

Musk oxen are surprisingly short, bison-like animals which live in large herds for protection from wolves. They are known for being extremely bad-tempered, charging at the slightest provocation, and covering snowy ground at incredible pace. The males also do battle over females, charging into each

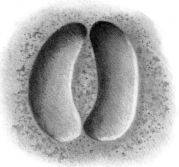

Musk ox footprint

other at great speed and crashing their heads together with a sickening clatter. Their cloven hooves create a print that is very round in profile.

If threatened by predators, musk oxen gather in a circle with any young at the centre.

TOP TIPS FOR A DEADLY DETECTIVE:
Lights in the night sky

In polar regions you may be lucky enough to see this incredible light show. The northern lights (aurora borealis) in the extreme north of the planet, and the southern lights (aurora australis) in the south are among nature's great wonders, with swirls of colour dancing across the night sky.

The colours are usually greens and golds, but occasionally you see reds and blues – every shade of the rainbow! This phenomenon is not easy to explain – it always gets my brain in a muddle trying to put it in simple language! Charged particles from the solar wind, a constant flow of particles from the sun beyond our atmosphere, are directed by the Earth's magnetic field towards the two poles. As these particles enter the atmosphere, they collide with other molecules, and energy and light are emitted.

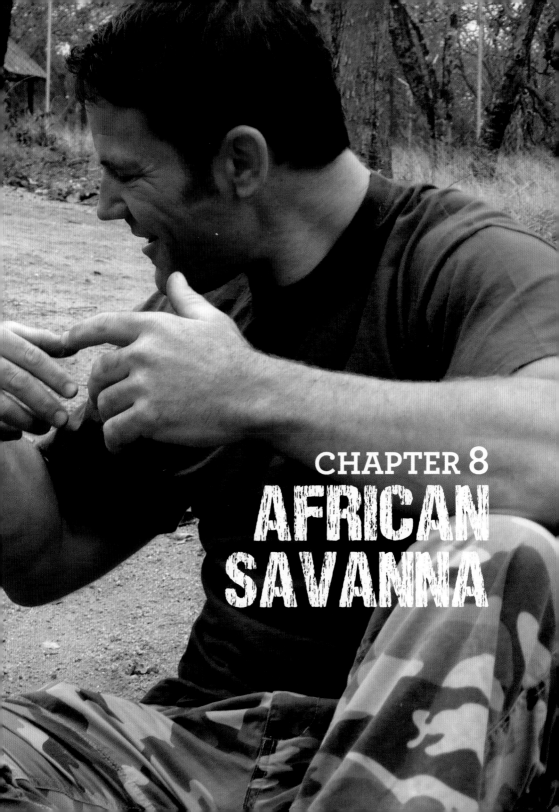

CHAPTER 8
AFRICAN SAVANNA

The great grasslands of Africa are the finest place on Earth to view big wildlife. But just because animals are big doesn't mean they're always easy to find. This is the most rewarding place to learn how to read animal signs because they're everywhere, and the animals you'll be interpreting are some of the most

A lion footprint in the sand.

exciting in the world. If you're ever lucky enough to go on a safari and drive into the bush to spot wildlife, spend at least some time looking not just out to the horizon, but also down

The great grasslands of Africa.

at the dirt along the side of the road. Once you've seen a lion print, you will never forget it. And just imagine how impressed everyone else on the tour will be if you spot them before your guide!

Q. *What is this?*

A. If I find picked clean bones outside a cave in Africa, two possible scenarios come to mind. The first is hyenas, which will sometimes bring back parts of their prey to their dens and may leave quite a mess outside. However, you would see their dog-like tracks in abundance around the entrance. The other is more curious. Porcupines (the biggest rodent in Africa, and probably second only in size to the capybara worldwide) are certainly not predators, but seem to love bones. They will drag them away from long-dead corpses and cache them both in and outside their homes. They gnaw on them to gain vital nutrients. On a much smaller scale, rodents such as mice may well gnaw on bones or discarded antlers they find in order to gain calcium. You can see their train track-like chewing marks on the bones.

Scratching posts
Cats need to keep their claws sharp, so will keep them sheathed for most of the working day. The sole exception is

A yawning lion. Big cats sleep for much of the day.

the cheetah – it keeps its claws extended in order to use them for traction, like an athlete's spiked running shoes. To keep their weaponry in extra fine fettle, cats sharpen their claws, usually on trees. With big cats like lions, this looks as though someone has taken a handful of chisels and raked them down the trunk. As the tiger can stand higher than any man, the rake marks are way up the tree.

More common is scratching from smaller cats, which may only rip the bark slightly. They can even completely shed the outer horny keratin coating of their claws in the process, which can very occasionally be found.

Bears, which live in other parts of the world, sharpen their claws too. It's also likely that they are spreading some of their own smell in the process, from scent glands between the claws. These can then be sniffed by other animals, letting them know who's in town.

Scent marking

We humans have a pathetic sense of smell compared to the animals around us. Bears, cats, dogs and other animals communicate to an extraordinary degree using smell, and often leave smells around deliberately for others to scratch and sniff at. I've watched a female tiger walking the length of her patch, spraying a powerhouse of pee up and down the bark of every prominent tree. And I've seen a coalition of two cheetah brothers rubbing their cheeks on every termite mound and tree stump that bordered their territory. The information found in that scent might merely tell others, 'Hey, there's another cheetah around.'

However, fresh scents, especially from scent-driven species, can tell any newcomer who cares to sniff the sex, age, dominance and health of the marking animal. Many

Cheetahs scratching and spraying to mark their territory.

animals, including members of the weasel family, have scent glands around the anus; others such as deer have them in their feet.

Making a camp in the bush

The African bush is one of the few places on earth where there are many large animals that can be dangerous to humans, and a number of those are active at night. If you ever need to camp out, you'll need to construct a rondevaal or boma. Go and find branches from thorny acacia bushes, then weave them together into a doughnut shape with your camp in the centre.

Prickly acacia branches help protect a camp in the bush.

Obviously the more branches you add, the safer your boma will be. Keeping a fire going all night will help to frighten away animals, and having someone on guard duty is a good idea too.

Q. *what is this?*

A. Male dung beetles roll poo into balls like these. A male was rolling this ball away to present to a female so she could lay her egg inside. However, torrential rains came at the wrong moment and the beetles dropped their load and scarpered. By the way, did you know that scientists have shown that dung beetles navigate at night using the light from the Milky Way? They proved it for certain by taking the insects into a planetarium and switching on and off various things in the night sky!

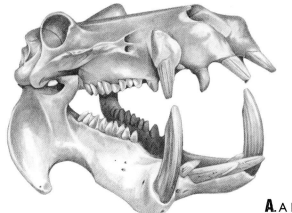

Looking for tracks.

Q. *What is this?*

A. A hippo skull.

Hippo sign

As large animals, hippos leave a lot of sign. During the day, they stay out of sight – you may only see their eyes, nostrils and ears above the water surface. However, at dusk they will come out to feed. You may see a well-worn path out of the water, with huge tracks. At the water's edge, a hippo may defecate, wagging its tail from side to side to spray dung onto nearby trees as a marker. The grass nearby will be cut as short as if someone had been through with a lawnmower. Take care to keep clear of these areas at dusk and through the night, and NEVER get between a hippo and the water, or between a mother and her calf.

Savanna giants

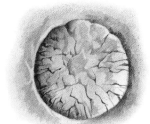

Front footprint of an elephant

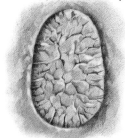

Back footprint

The giant footprints of an elephant are unmistakable.

Elephants are the largest land mammals. The biggest on record was shot in Angola, had feet as wide as dustbin lids, and weighed around 10 tonnes! Obviously an animal this size is a treasure to track. An elephant walks on its toes and the rear part of its foot is a dense fatty pad that cushions the vast weight of the animal. The front track is circular. By measuring around the print, you can estimate the size of an elephant – it is roughly twice as high at the shoulder as the circumference of the front foot.

I get too close to a pile of elephant poo!

Elephants also leave lots of sign of their presence. They smash down trees to get at the forage in the canopy above, and will leave total destruction in their path. Over time, they have been one of the great architects of the savanna, creating grasslands that otherwise might have grown over with trees. They are one of many animals that visit 'salt licks'. They eat these mineral deposits to settle an upset stomach, or provide things that are otherwise missing in their diets.

Animal horns

Horns and antlers may look similar but they are fundamentally different. Antlers, seen on animals such as deer, are made of bone. Each year they are shed, then grow again for use in battles over mates. They are covered with skin and soft hair known as velvet.

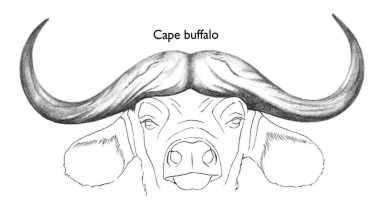

Cape buffalo

Horns, seen on animals such as cattle, buffalo and antelope, are made of bone covered with keratin – the same substance as our fingernails and hair. There are lots of different shapes but they are not branched like antlers. Horns are not shed and in many species they keep on growing throughout the animal's life.

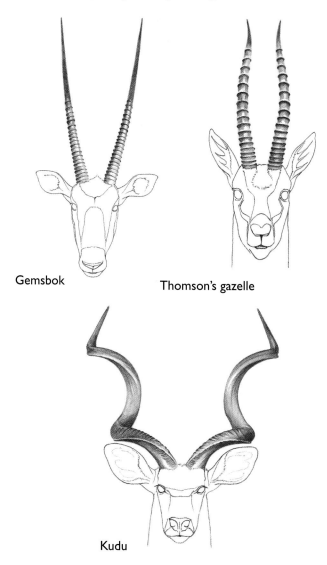

Gemsbok

Thomson's gazelle

Kudu

A scorpion leaves its track in the desert sand.

When hunting for scorpions you can narrow your search by looking out for the bleached rings left behind when they've been feeding on millipedes. You can also look out for the moults of scorpions, left behind when the animal has climbed out of its old skin to grow.

Scorpions like to hunt millipedes and these rings are the leftovers from a scorpion's meal.

///// THE CASE OF: /////
THE CROCS AND HIPPOS

The Okavango Delta is the perfect place to film wildlife,
with elephant, lion and kudu charging through the waters
and allowing your boat to get much closer than
you would ever dare on foot.

On a recent trip I went there to dive in the pools with
Nile crocodiles. It's one of the most edgy wildlife encounters on
the planet and even a few years ago it would have been totally
unthinkable. However, local wildlife expert Brad Besterlink has
worked out that in the winter the water is cool enough that
even the big crocs are not really interested in attacking.

Even so, as I entered the water I have to admit to being utterly
terrified. As we swam along the bottom into the pool, I saw a drag
mark through the sand, the unmistakable slice of a croc's tail. The
flow had not yet broken it down, so it was relatively fresh.
I realised that the animal could well be in the pool ahead.
I forced myself to be calm, to reduce my heart rate;
the last thing you want with a wild animal is to be scared
as they can sense fear. But as we swam into the pond,
something happened that we certainly weren't planning.

Along the bottom we found a completely different set of prints.
They were as round as dinner plates, and perhaps as deep as my
little finger. Hippo! Now this is an animal you would not want to
encounter on a scuba dive.

To my knowledge, nobody had ever dived with one; they are simply
the most angry and unpredictable animal in Africa and there's an
oft-repeated quote that they kill more people here than any other
creature. To swim into one would be totally unthinkable.

Just as we decided to turn and get out of there, a great grey shape lumbered from the murk. The breath caught in the back of my throat. The hippo was probably a young male. He baulked as he caught sight of us, turned slowly and then moved away. At the closest point he was no more than two metres away from us.

We all raced to exit the water, breathing hard with exertion and fear. It was one moment where a little more Deadly Detective work beforehand could have saved us a lot of terror!

CHAPTER 9
TROPICAL RAINFOREST

Though the tropical rainforest is the most biodiverse of all environments – that is, most loaded with life – it can be a surprisingly tough place to track down animals. Mouldy leaf litter won't hold a track, many animals only come out at night, and others choose to stick to the treetops, fly, or use waterways to get around. In the jungle, naturalists have to adapt their techniques to track down forest creatures such as coati, agouti, tapir and jaguar.

Coati footprint

Tapir footprint

Look out for bent grasses or disturbed undergrowth that tell of an animal that would otherwise remain elusive. These may well lead you to fruiting or flowering trees which function like waterholes on the African savanna, drawing in animals from miles around.

Jaguar footprint

Camera traps

Sometimes it is just not possible to sit for hours next to a carcass or an animal's den and hope the owner turns up. Apart from anything else, having a noisy, smelly human sitting nearby is likely to frighten off any really sensitive animal. In this situation, we often use camera traps. Over recent years these have become smaller, more affordable and easier to set up. The real knack, though, to

Agouti footprint

Practising with my camera trap in England.

camera trapping is learning to think like the animal you are trying to film. I reckon tigers are the animals we've had the finest results with, but it's a real challenge getting yourself into the mindset of the world's largest cat. The best thing to do is to put cameras on well-established game trails, around the scratching posts they use to mark their territories, and in any obvious river crossings that a self-respecting big cat would use.

159

White-nosed coati.

THE CASE OF:
THE CHIMPANZEE

For me, chimpanzees are the most exciting primate to film.
They do so much in a single day, alternating from frantically
screaming and yelling while hurling themselves hand over
hand through the treetops, to sitting quietly grooming each other
or feeding on fruit. They also hunt monkeys and small antelope,
which is a truly chilling sight to behold.

Finding chimpanzees has always required a lot of Deadly Detective
work. The first time I went after them was in Uganda nearly a
decade ago. We set off shortly before dawn, wandering down small
paths into the dark forest. The first sign we came across was poo.
It was remarkably human in appearance and in pong – stinky!
Most of it was made up of sticky fruit and little seeds, showing that
the animals had been feeding on figs. Our guide said he knew of a
fig tree perhaps a mile away that was bearing fruit, so we changed
course and headed towards it. Twenty minutes farther on we
crossed a small stream; the soft mud at one side held a print that
was clearly the fingers of a clenched fist, which had been laid just
minutes before. Breathing in, we noticed that the musty scent of
the animal itself was still heavy in the air.

At that second, there was a manic scream, building in intensity:
the classic chimp long call. The chimps had already left the forest
floor and were stampeding around in the treetops several hundred
metres away. We'd been sneaking in so quietly and carefully,
trying not to do anything that might scare them away, but now we
grabbed our cameras and tripod and ran, desperate to get to
the chimps before they disappeared.

When we reached them, they were up in the fig tree, fighting over who got to eat the best figs. It was chaos, with younger animals being beaten and screamed at for daring to approach the best clumps of fruit. We followed the chimps all day as they bounced down from the treetops and loped along the ground, looking like sinister cavemen with their hunched shoulders and bald heads. It was one of the most life-changing experiences I have ever had, and would never have occurred without some Deadly Detective work.

Q. *What caused this?*

A. These pieces of leaf were made by leaf-cutter ants. They were carrying them back to their nest when it started to rain really heavily. The ants ran for cover, dropping the leaves behind them. On one memorable occasion in Costa Rica, the ants had been collecting slices of a pink flower and the rains had made them drop them. It looked as if someone had laid a trail of petals for a miniature bride!

Crocodile nests

For me the most exciting sign left behind by any animal are the nests of crocodilians. There are 23 different species of crocodile, and they all have subtly different nesting strategies. The saltwater crocodile, for example, will gather a nest of rotting vegetation and lay her eggs inside it. As the big compost heap decomposes it gets warm and keeps the eggs at a stable temperature.

Nile crocodiles, on the other hand, dig into sand banks and bury their forty or so eggs inside. The best way of finding one of these nests is to look out for the

Crocodile with her nest and eggs.

distinctive drag marks made by the female as she comes out
of the water to keep an eye on her nest. You'll see very evident

Drag marks left by a crocodile tail.

165

Crocodile front footprint

Back footprint

tail marks, strongly clawed toes and maybe the imprint of her belly scales on the ground where she's lain close to the nest to bask while guarding her eggs. If you prod your finger into the sand, you may find an area that's slightly softer than the rest because it's been dug over.

If ever I do look inside a croc nest I make sure I return the eggs exactly as I found them. They must be orientated the right way to keep the baby croc inside safe. I always take real care around such a nest, as mother crocs are intensely maternal and will give their lives to protect their young. An angry female croc is not to be trifled with.

Droppings

A crocodile's droppings look quite unlike those of any other animal. They are usually uniformly coloured, very pale or maybe white, and like a lump of chalk. The crocodile's digestive acids are so intense that there is rarely anything recognisable in the droppings.

Q. *Do you know the collective noun for these animals?*

Hippos   **A.** a bloat or pod
Rhinos   **A.** a crash
Crows   **A.** a murder
Goldfish   **A.** a troubling
Lions   **A.** a pride
Cheetahs   **A.** a coalition
Goldfinches   **A.** a charm
Herons   **A.** a sedge or siege
Owls   **A.** a parliament
Goats   **A.** a trip, tribe or herd
Frogs   **A.** an army
Larks   **A.** an exultation

This is a spider moult. As they grow, spiders must shed their old outer layer (exoskeleton) to reveal the new, larger one.

THE CASE OF:
THE MIGHTY SNAKE

On an expedition in Borneo, I found myself searching for snakes in
the oil palm plantations alongside the area of forest we were trying
to get protected. I'd spent many months travelling the area and
spoke the local language fairly well, so set to questioning some of
the workers who lived there. Pretty soon I started building up
a picture that there was at least one really big snake that
had been coming into one of the settlements and raiding their
chicken coops. When I asked where they thought the snake lived,
the locals responded, 'Bukit Gaja': elephant hill!

Bukit Gaja was an overgrown jumble of immense boulders tangled
with vines and dense vegetation. The locals refused to go there,
as it was an old tribal burial ground. Indeed, when we penetrated
through the undergrowth we found several ironwood coffins, green
with mould, and a few human bones and skulls. Much more exciting,
though, was the fact that the hill was peppered with holes and
caves, the perfect hiding spot for a monster snake.

We scoured the place thoroughly and finally found some holes
with the rocks below them rubbed so smooth it looked as if
they had been polished over decades. This had to be down to the
movements of the belly scales of a big snake. For two nights we
waited there in total darkness until sunrise, hoping for a slithering
sound in the dry leaves. Nothing, apart from us all
getting thoroughly spooked and covered in mosquito bites.
But on the final day, just as we were leaving the plantation,
one of the locals flagged us down and told us that their
chicken pen had been raided the night before.

We followed the slithering marks in the dirt and when they ran
out, I tried to put myself into the snake's shoes – so to speak!

Where would it go? Water was the obvious answer. Big pythons like to travel by water as it supports their bulk. Under a bridge over a nearby stream, we found our prize: a four-metre long reticulated python stuffed full of chicken dinner. It lunged at me several times before splashing into the water, but I grabbed it just in time. To make sure the snake came to no harm we took it out into the forest where there was plenty of prey and it could live the rest of its life safely. Again, a little Detective work saved the day.

I've been handling snakes my whole life, and study them obsessively, yet sometimes I still look at a snake and think, 'What is that?!' It is all too easy to get caught out. Please, please don't consider picking up a wild snake unless you have had many years of experience and training. A venomous snake bite is always unpleasant, but can be fatal.

CHAPTER 10
DESERT

The desert may appear to be totally barren, but at night it comes alive. Small patches of grass may have been daytime home to invertebrates such as spiders, crickets and ants. Some reptiles will bury themselves under the sand where it is cooler and potentially damp, emerging at night to feed. The best – and sometimes the only – way of locating these animals is to look for the story they leave behind in the dunes.

Night tracks

The best way to see a print in the sand is when shadows are cast across it. During the middle of the day when direct sunlight is shining straight down, prints are near invisible. Dusk and dawn are brilliant as the low sun casts long shadows – and this is the most pleasant time to be in the desert

Caracal footprint

anyway. At night, bend down to the sand, put your torch down to ground level and cast the light across the top of a print; this will make it much more obvious.

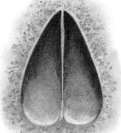

Oryx footprint

Water in the desert

While some desert animals, including the Arabian oryx and the kangaroo rat, can go most of their lives without drinking water, most mammals (including humans) need to drink regularly. Being able to find water could make the difference between life and death. On dune systems near the coast, damp air may blow across the sands first thing in the morning. Look out for tenebrionid beetles, which will run to the highest point around, then stand with their bottoms up in the air. Water condenses on them

Hyena footprints

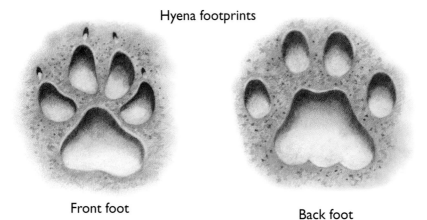

Front foot

Back foot

and trickles down into their mouths. You can try the same method using scarves and other clothing, hanging them where the beetles stand and then wringing the moisture out.

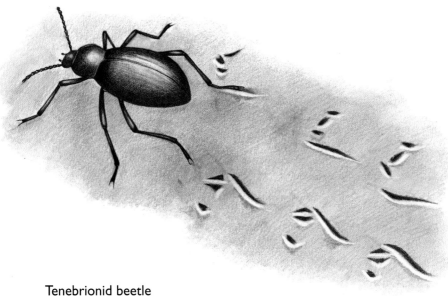

Tenebrionid beetle
and its tracks in the sand.

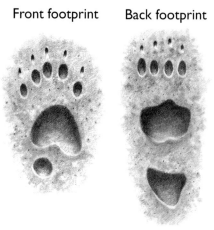

A numbat and its footprint.

Australian desert dwellers have a range of ways of coping with lack of water and extreme heat. The numbat, a small carnivorous marsupial, gets the water it needs from the thousands of termites it eats every day. In the middle of the day it shelters from the heat in an underground burrow. Kangaroos cool themselves by licking their forearms which have lots of blood vessels close to the skin. As the saliva evaporates the blood is cooled, lowering the animal's body temperature. A kangaroo may also scrape away baking hot earth to lie on the cooler soil beneath and you may spot signs of this.

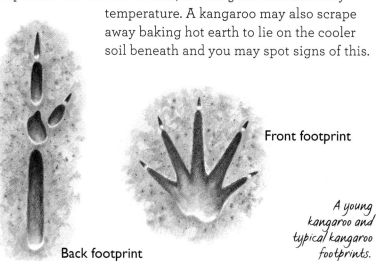

Front footprint

Back footprint

A young kangaroo and typical kangaroo footprints.

DEADLY DETECTIVES

A thorny devil has ridges on its body that help direct tiny water droplets to the corner of its mouth.

///// THE CASE OF: //////

THE SPOOR SPIDER

Most tracking involves vertebrates – large mammals, reptiles and birds – but even the itty-bitty things can be tracked with the right know-how. In Namibia, we found lines of tiny markings in the sand, leading to a clump of grasses. There we saw two tiny semi-circular bumps. I quickly took a handful of the sand and blew away the excess grains to reveal a beautiful tiny spider – the spoor spider.

'Spoor' is the word many Africans use to describe a track and the markings in the soil looked much like a mini-version of the spoor of a buffalo. This incredible little creature weaves itself a blanket of silk, pulls some sand onto it, then lies underneath, hidden from view. When an ant wanders nearby, the spider reaches out and clamps the ant down to the surface of the sand, which is so hot that the ant cooks to death! After I'd had a little look at the spider I dropped him safely down again. As I watched, he flipped over on to his back, wove a blanket with swift movements of the legs over his spinnerets, then slipped under it. Magic!

TOP TIPS FOR A DEADLY DETECTIVE: Dealing with snakebites!

The first rule with a snakebite is to get to hospital as soon as you can, but if you're miles out in the desert that's not always possible. Here are some simple rules to follow if you are bitten by a snake and you cannot get help.

1. ID the snake without putting yourself at risk of another bite. A photo, or well-taken notes of size, colour and identifying marks, will be useful later.
2. Modern snakebite advice says you should not attempt to suck venom out of a wound. Cutting open the wound is a very bad idea.
3. Bind over the wound with a pressure bandage, but do not use a tourniquet.
4. Don't panic. Getting overwrought brings up your breathing and heart rate, which speeds the flow of venom around the body. Also, if you can reduce the physical effort you need to get to safety (for instance, be carried on a stretcher), then do it.
5. Don't ever handle snakes unless you are experienced. The majority of snakebites in the Western world come from inexperienced people messing with snakes.

Q. *What do you think laid this trail?*

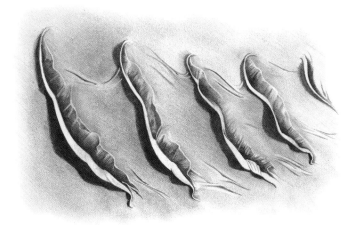

A. A sidewinder snake.

Firestarter

The skill of making a fire and disposing of it correctly is essential for any outdoors expert, but it is one that must be learned properly and practised responsibly. Fire can obviously be dangerous to us, but that is nothing compared to the effects of a wildfire that can ravage an environment and cause chaos. Many places that are susceptible to wildfires will have warning systems in place that tell you when it is unacceptable to light a fire.

Round a campfire.

Making fire depends on the fire triangle: you need fuel, oxygen and heat. The most effective and hottest fires will have a way for air to get beneath them. Too much wind, however, is not good,

THE CASE OF:

THE SIDEWINDER

In the deserts of Namibia lives a remarkable snake which gets around on the dunes by means of a dazzling method of locomotion: sidewinding. The Peringuey's adder is fairly small and buries itself in the sand during the heat of the day, making it totally invisible. The only way you can find it is by searching out the tracks it makes as it winds across the sands.

The team and I started out at first light, before the wind could obliterate the essential trace of our desert snake. We split up so we could cover as much ground as humanly possible in our search, and spent several hours with nothing at all, yomping through the dunes in vain. Finally, just as we were nearing the moment when we'd have to give in, I heard the cameraman yelling and I raced towards him. Running up the side of a dune was a line of tracks that looked like elongated 'S' shapes. At the end of them, buried in the less compact sand at the base of a clump of grasses, was our snake. We would never have found it without some good old-fashioned tracking.

so building a hearth around the site using rocks will help. Don't take rocks from rivers, as they may explode in the heat.

First, form a small bundle of your most flammable material to make tinder. Paper, wool, scrapings of silver birch bark and fungus are all excellent tinder. Over this, arrange a tepee of small kindling such as twigs or bark, dry palm leaves or heather, cardboard or woodchips.

Have your main fuel source to hand before you start the fire. Light a small corner of the exposed tinder and gently blow on it to generate an ember or flame. Directly expose the small kindling, then gradually build up the size of the fuel over the growing flames.

When you are ready to move on from your fire, it is essential to completely douse any embers. If you are in the desert it's unlikely you'll have enough water to do this, so spread the embers as wide as possible and scatter sand over them. Be warned that if you do this over the embers while they're still concentrated you will just keep the heat blazing below the surface, and also that a single windborne ember can start a wildlife that could cause absolute chaos. So KILL YOUR FIRE!

Some snakes give birth to live young, others lay eggs.
I found these long after they had hatched.

CHAPTER 11
MARINE

The ocean may seem like the environment where Deadly Detective work is of least use. After all, water is constantly changing and its surface doesn't hold a trail – surely this is a place where encounters with animals just happen rather than you seeking them out with your tracking skills? However, I'd like to argue that there are plenty of ways to be an oceanic investigator, and some of these skills could also keep you alive.

Not everyone is lucky enough to be able to go scuba diving like we do when filming Deadly, but there are plenty of signs of marine life you can spot from the shore or a boat if you know what to look for. Watch for whale spouts – the clouds of condensed water vapour visible when the whale surfaces and breathes out through one or more blowholes on the top of its head. You may also spot whale tail flukes or their dorsal fins. Also, get to know the shapes of seabirds and you will be able to identify them as they glide over the ocean.

I encounter a Humboldt squid while diving.

Spouts

Grey whale: broad spout
from two blowholes

Sperm whale: spout is at an
angle, from one blowhole on
the left of the head

Blue whale: tall column
up to 12 metres high

Orcas are expert predators which hunt alone and in groups.

Tail flukes

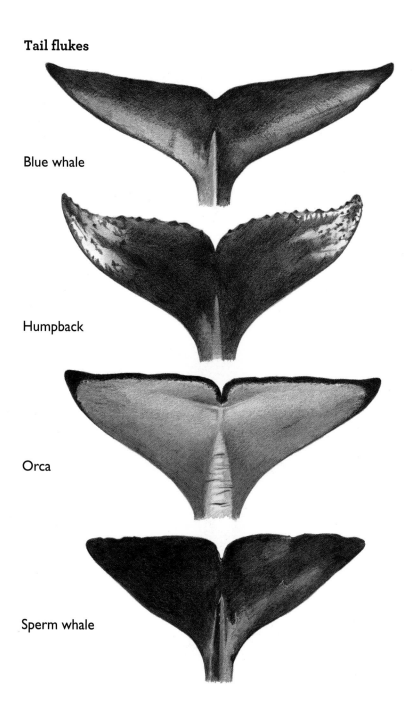

Blue whale

Humpback

Orca

Sperm whale

Dorsal fins

Pilot whale

Dall's porpoise

Minke whale

Orca

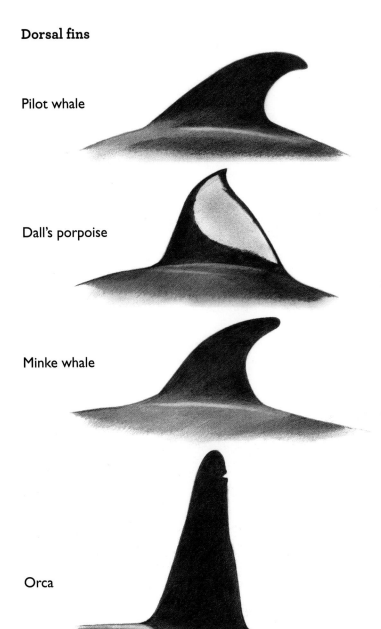

THE CASE OF: THE SPERM WHALE

Sperm whales are arguably the largest predator ever to have lived. They're certainly the biggest toothed animal on earth, have the biggest brain of any animal, are the deepest diving creature, can hold their breath for the longest time. However, despite their size, looking for a sperm whale in the ocean would be like searching for a needle in a haystack, were it not for the fact that they also make the loudest sounds of any animal.

Sperm whales make a variety of different sounds, some for communication, others to locate prey. Some are even so powerful that they can be used to stun prey. It's believed that an adult male sperm whale can generate 220 decibels of noise, which would be like standing right next to a fighter jet as it took off!

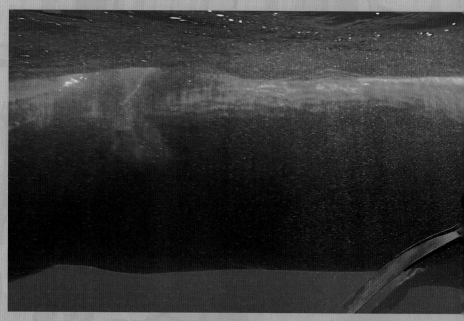

It's easy to hear these sounds from many miles away using a hydrophone, a highly directional waterproofed microphone. By listening to where the sounds are loudest you can home in on the whales themselves. Off the island of Dominica we tracked down small groups of whales with the aim of filming them underwater. Many of them just weren't interested in us and swam on, ignoring us completely, but every so often an animal would turn and swim right towards me. On one occasion, a female with her calf was doing barrel rolls so close to me I could have run my hand down her flank. On another occasion, a young male started to rub his head on our boat as if he was having a scratch. You can hear the clicks they are making in the water as they chatter to each other, but as an animal turns to face you and you are staring down the barrel of its massive nose, the clicks become so intense that you can feel them resonating through your whole body.

Sea bird ID

Frigate birds glide on stiff wings, barely ever flapping.

Puffins beat their wings like clockwork toys, their bodies seemingly round and way too big for their wings. They will often float in rafts with thousands of other puffins.

Pelicans usually fly close to the surface of the sea, using the fact that wind is driven upwards by the waves.

Albatrosses can glide for hours with scarcely a flap of their long wings.

Storm petrels are tiny for seabirds. They may seem to dance on the water, probably enticing small fish and crustaceans to the surface.

THE GIANT PACIFIC OCTOPUS

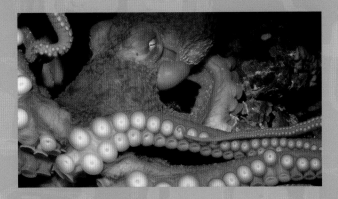

In the coastal seas off Vancouver Island in Canada, I was on the hunt for the giant Pacific octopus, the largest of all octopus species. It's a phenomenal beast and there are tales of divers being engulfed in animals that seem like vast flapping duvets. In order to find them, though, you have to follow underwater clues.

Diving in among the kelp, we kept our eyes peeled for scattered pieces of crab shell which had been pulled apart by these predators. Often we'd come across a big pile of shell chunks in front of a crack in the rocks, the octopus's den. One such den had an animal inside. He had an arm that was as thick as my leg, but he was too cautious to come out and say hello. However, on our very last dive, we found another octopus sitting in the entrance to its den. It had a totally different character and came out quite happily onto the sea floor, seeming to enjoy contact with my bare fingers. After teasing its arm tips over my mask and wetsuit, it dragged itself over the bottom and away to hunt. It was an extraordinary experience, but this octopus (which had an arm span wider than me) only had arms about as thick as a soft drink can. It's tantalising to think quite how enormous the octopus that stayed hidden must have been.

Sargassum and FADs

In the open sea, any tiny piece of floating debris becomes a focus for activity. Mats of seagrass called sargassum, and nowadays accumulations of garbage left by humans, attract fish from miles and miles around, which shelter beneath them. Larger fish such as sharks come here to feed on the smaller ones, so these can be sensational places to pop in and dive or snorkel. Increasingly, fishermen are exploiting this habit in fish, creating artificial Floating Attraction Devices or FADs. They may be rafts of plastic barrels tied together and anchored on very long lines to the bottom. Fishermen could trawl lines over miles of open sea and find nothing, but simply dragging a line past an FAD will always yield results.

Q. In a kelp forest, there is a hole in the rocks, and outside it is a litter pile of crab shells. What made it?

A. These have been made by a giant Pacific octopus, which tears crabs apart with its intensely strong arms, then munches them with its hard beak.

Q. In the same kelp forest, there are remains of crabs, urchins, abalone and mussels, but they are scattered over a large area and totally shattered. What did this?

A. This is the work of a sea otter. They carry a flat stone which they use as an anvil, placing prey on their chests and smashing it open.

Q. There is a large patch of coral reef that is completely white and non-living. There is no evidence of pollution. What caused it?

A. Many things can kill off coral, including rising sea temperatures, pollution run-off from the land, and attack by other corals. However in this case this was the work of the crown of thorns, a venomous starfish which throws up its stomach over the corals and digests them. A plague of crown of thorns will completely destroy a reef.

Kelp forests are home to a wide range of marine creatures.

////// THE CASE OF: //////
THE GREAT WHITE

I guess it's not surprising that great white sharks have been
on my filming schedule so often. They are most people's idea
of what Deadly really means, despite the fact that they only
kill an average of one person a year in the whole world.
In South Africa, the sharks have a unique way of catching
their prey, powering up from deep water almost vertically
in order to hit seals at the surface. They are travelling
so fast that they breach beyond the waves, their massive
bodies flying completely clear of the water.

This happens every day in the cold waters near an island
where seals are known to hang out, but it's impossible to
predict where it's going to happen – unless you use a little
brain power.

The great whites detect the seals at the surface
using a combination of sight and motion detection
from the organ known as the lateral line, which runs
down the length of their body. If you can recreate
the impression of a seal moving on the surface,
you can trick the sharks into breaching.

We towed a decoy behind our boat – a chunk of wetsuit
material cut into the shape of a baby seal, a great white's
favourite food! It took just minutes for our first shark to
hit the bait and fly out of the water, captured beautifully on
high-speed camera. Absolutely extraordinary and all made
possible by experience, planning . . . and a little
Deadly Detective work!

INDEX

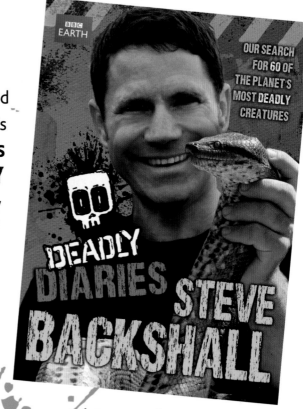